Macmillan Profes

Macmillan Professional Masters

Titles in the series

Company Accounts Roger Oldcorn
Constitutional and Administrative Law John Alder
Contract Law Ewan McKendrick
Cost and Management Accounting Roger Hussey
Criminal Law Marise Cremona
Data Processing John Bingham
Employee Relations Chris Brewster
Land Law Kate Green
Landlord and Tenant Law Margaret Wilkie and Godfrey Cole
Management Roger Oldcorn
Marketing Robert G. I. Maxwell
Office Administration E. C. Eyre
Personnel Management Margaret Attwood
Study Skills Kate Williams
Supervision Mike Savedra and John Hawthorn

Company Accounts

Roger Oldcorn

Deputy Director of the Management Development and Advisory Service at Henley – The Management College

First published by Pan Books Ltd in 1984 as
Understanding Company Accounts
in the Breakthrough series.

Fully updated and revised edition published by
MACMILLAN EDUCATION LTD
Houndmills, Basingstoke, Hampshire RG21 2XS
and London
Companies and representatives
throughout the world

Typeset by TecSet Ltd, Wallington, Surrey

Printed in the People's Republic of China

British Library Cataloguing in Publication Data
Oldcorn, Roger
Company accounts.—Updated and rev. ed.
1. Companies. Accounts
I. Title II. Oldcorn, Roger (Understanding
company accounts)
657.95
ISBN 0–333–48792–3
ISBN 0–333–48793–1 Pbk
ISBN 0–333–48794–X Pbk export

Contents

Acknowledgements

The author and publishers wish to thank United Biscuits (Holdings) PLC for giving permission to reproduce so much of the company's annual report and accounts, and also Marks and Spencer plc for permission to reproduce the statement on p. 79.

Introduction

This book has been written for anyone who needs to understand and use company accounts, especially those who do not want (nor have any desire) to become accountants. Its purpose is to explain accounting statements to the layman – to translate the language of finance – and to show the reader how to study the accounts for clues about the organization, its efficiency and its effectiveness.

Accounting statements have improved out of all recognition during the last twenty years and, as far as published company accounts are concerned, now contain a great deal of useful information. Similarly, there has been a tremendous upsurge in the number of people who 'need to know' about companies in greater depth and more objectively than is provided by a few short paragraphs in the financial newspapers. The list of types of people who have a more than passing interest in companies is quite lengthy: it is not just the owners or shareholders who need to know, but employees (and prospective employees), bankers, other lenders, customers, suppliers and all others who feel that, at least if you understand it, you will know better how to behave towards it. Most of these people are not accountants, yet the bulk of 'hard' information about a company comes in the form of accounting statements. Is it any wonder that companies are misunderstood, that well-run firms do not always receive the recognition due to them, and that poor companies can get away with their inefficiencies for a long time? Also, is it surprising that so many small firms go out of business after trading for only a year or two? All the warning signs will have been there in the accounts; lack of understanding in these circumstances is fatal.

In this book I have concentrated on the accounting information that is usually made available to the public ('published accounts'). If you are inside the business, more information is available to you and, if you have a special interest in a firm (like the bank manager), you will need more information than the accounts themselves provide. Even so, the published accounts are an excellent starting point for anyone who wants to understand.

How to Use this Book

The chapters in this book follow on from each other in a logical fashion and ideas in any particular chapter may have been introduced in earlier chapters. It is not very easy therefore to dip in and out of the book at random; treat it more like one long novel than a series of short stories.

You should have a notebook and pencil to hand, for jotting down interesting points or questions and for somewhere to work out the puzzles that appear from time to time. You will need either to have a small calculator or to be able to add, subtract, multiply, divide and work out percentages without too much bother. There is no involved mathematics.

Throughout the book you will find questions which you should try to answer before reading on; they are designed to test your understanding of what has just been discussed, or to introduce a new topic.

Part I describes the different accounting documents in some detail, explaining technical words as they occur. Generally, however, technical explanations have been avoided – for example, there is no detailed explanation of either corporation tax or how tax on dividends works. The reading list at the end of the book directs you to detailed texts on technical topics. Part II shows how accounts can be evaluated and, generally, I have only referred to information that is shown in the published accounts. The exception is the discussion of ratios that use stock market prices. This is for completeness and because the information is easily available. The whole world of the interpretation of 'management accounts' is outside the scope of the book.

Part I

Accounting Statements – What are They and What are They for?

1 What the Different Statements are for

The purpose of company accounts is to present information about a company's affairs in financial terms and should enable the reader to answer two very basic questions about it – first, how has it managed its affairs over a period of time? and second, what is its current financial situation? To be able to answer these questions information is needed about such things as the company's level of sales, the costs it has incurred, the profit it has made, how much money it has and from where it has obtained its finance.

The main sources of information are the documents known as 'the profit and loss account', 'the source and application of funds' and 'the balance sheet', although companies have to provide other information as well.

These documents are not a new invention; they have been developing over hundreds of years and all over the world similar accounting statements will be found.

To illustrate what these documents contain, consider the case of the small business called Uncle Percy's Car Sales. Uncle Percy is a self-employed car salesman, operating a very simple business. On the first day of each month he receives a delivery of ten cars which he stores in his back yard and tries to sell them. Each car he buys costs him £4800 and he always sells them for £5000 each. Clearly Uncle Percy makes a profit of £200 on every car he sells. So if he sells two cars his profit is £400. If he sells three he makes £600, and so on. In other words, if he sells all ten cars that are delivered each month he makes a profit of £2000.

1.1 A Working Definition of 'Profit'

From what I have described about Uncle Percy's Car Sales, you will see that profit has something to do with what has been sold and the cost involved in the sale. We can define profit therefore as: the difference between the value of what has been sold and the costs associated with sales. Notice that it is *not* the cost of what was bought that is important here, nor the cost of what was made (if the business had been manufacturing cars). The important thing to work out is the cost of what was sold. This is a very simple definition of profit; we will look at it in more detail later, defining the word 'cost' very carefully (see Chapter 5). So

profit is:

the price something is sold for	price
minus the costs incurred in making the sale	costs
Equals	profit

Self-check

If Uncle Percy had only been able to sell the cars for £4500 each, and the cost to him stayed the same at £4800 how much profit would he have made on each car sold?

This is, of course, a trick question. If we use the definition of profit above, the cost is more than the price. In fact the cost is £300 more than the price. In the language of accountants, Uncle Percy would not have made a profit at all, but a *loss*.

1.2 **Profit and Loss**

A few weeks ago Uncle Percy told me that he had enjoyed a very successful month's trading, so I asked him to describe what had happened.

'As usual,' he said, 'ten cars were delivered on the first of the month and the cost price was the normal £4800. I had no difficulty at all in selling all ten cars at the normal selling price of £5000. By my reckoning', he went on, 'I made a profit of £2000.'

I agreed with him by saying that, if he managed to sell ten cars at £200 profit a car, he certainly had made £2000 profit. If, however, we had asked an accountant to describe what had been going on, he would have prepared a statement which he would have called a 'profit and loss account'.

Accountants like to set things out neatly and in their own special way, and, in the case of Uncle Percy's Car Sales, this is how it might look:

Uncle Percy's Car Sales – Profit and Loss Account
for month ending 31 January 1989

Sales 10 cars at £5000 each	£50 000
Less cost of cars sold (10 cars at £4800)	£48 000
Profit	£2000

Activity

On a separate piece of paper write out a profit and loss account statement for Uncle Percy assuming that he had managed to sell only eight cars during the month. The selling price is £5000 as before and the cost is £4800, also as before. Set the account out in the same way as it was presented above.

Did you work out that the profit on eight cars would have been £1600? Your profit and loss account should look something like this:

Sales 8 cars at £5000 each	£40 000
Less cost of cars sold (8 cars at £4800)	£38 400
Profit	£1 600

You could have checked your answer by using the short cut we used earlier – if Uncle Percy had managed to sell eight cars at a profit of £200 each, then he certainly made a total profit of £1600.

There are three points to note in relation to the profit and loss accounts just set out. First, the period of time to which the figures relate must always be shown. In this case the account relates to a month which finished on 31 January 1989.

The second point is that, sometimes, this sort of statement is called a 'trading account' because it describes the trading activities of the business over a period of time. The precise difference between the two names will be explained in Chapter 5.

Thirdly, real profit and loss accounts for real companies are much more complicated than these examples. However, no matter how involved they seem, their purpose is basically the same.

1.3 What About the Money?

You might think that Uncle Percy has a very easy time of it and does not have any worries. After all, he has merely to sell cars and, on every one he sells, he makes a profit. This is true but there is a snag, and that is the problem of money. The way his business works is more involved than you might think. The people who supply him with cars have a rule which states that all cars delivered during a month have to be paid for on the last day of the month, whether or not they have been sold. So Uncle Percy has to pay out the full cost of all ten cars at the end of the month even if he has not sold any of them. For example, in the month of January 1989, Uncle Percy received a total of £50 000 from the sales of the cars in his yard. On 31 January he sent off a cheque to the suppliers for £48 000 which was the cost price of the ten cars. No matter what happens, the cheque for £48 000 has to be sent on the last day of the month.

Activity

Suppose Uncle Percy started the month of February with no money in hand or in the bank. How much money would he have at the end of the month if he only sold eight cars at £5000 each, he paid for all ten (at a total cost of £48 000) and he spent no other money during the month?

You will probably have worked out by now why Uncle Percy does not lead a worry-free life. The fact is that if he only sells eight cars in a month, he receives only £40 000 yet he has to pay out £48 000. This would put him in an awkward situation. Not only would he have nothing to live on, but the bank manager would refuse to pay the cheque (making Uncle Percy broke) or would charge him a lot of money in interest for being what is usually called 'overdrawn' or 'in the red'.

Once again, if we had asked an accountant to describe what had been going on as far as the money is concerned, he would have prepared a statement which he would have called 'a cash flow statement'. Various other names are given to this statement including:

- Source and application of funds.
- Movement of funds.
- Source and disposition of funds.
- Source and use of funds.

As far as Uncle Percy's business is concerned, the statement would look like this:

Statement of source and use of funds for month ending 28 February 1989

Receipts Sales of cars (8 at £5000)	£40 000
Payments Purchases (10 cars at £4800)	£48 000
Cash surplus or (deficit)	(£8 000)

You will have noticed that the word 'deficit' has been put in brackets, as well as the number itself. This is another accountants' habit – actually they call it a 'convention' – whenever the calculation results in a minus answer, it is put in a bracket or in red ink. Hence the expression 'in the red', meaning more money has gone out than came in.

The other point to note is that these statements tend to be very complicated indeed in real firms, but all of them show three things:

- where the money came from;
- where the money went to;
- how the difference was handled.

1.4 The Basic Business Problem – Money and Profit are not the Same

In the example above we imagined that Uncle Percy managed to sell only eight cars in February 1989. This put him £8000 in the red. However, you have already worked out how much profit he would have made on that level of sales (see p. 5). He made a profit of £1600 on those eight cars yet he ended up with a severe shortage of money. We know that he has two cars still unsold in his back yard but that does not solve his immediate problem – what is he going to live on until he sells another car?

This is one of the problems which besets all business organisations large or small – it is difficult to produce a reasonable profit and, at the same time, have enough money to keep going. In a nutshell: profit and money are never the same (only by accident).

There are many reasons why the balance of money at the end of a period of time may not be the same as the amount of profit made. The example we have been working on is the situation where purchases are more than receipts from sales. Here are two more examples – try to work out the money balance in each case:

1 Uncle Percy decided to sell two cars 'on credit'. This meant that the customers bought the cars but did not actually pay for them there and then. They signed a note to the effect that they owed Uncle Percy £5000 each. During the same month the other eight cars were sold for cash. So the profit for the month was £2000 and as usual a cheque went to the suppliers for £48 000.

Self-check

How much money was in the bank (or overdrawn) at the end?

---

2 On another occasion, Uncle Percy decided to pay the supplier for only eight of the ten cars that had been delivered. During the month he sold all ten cars at a profit of £2000 as usual, for cash, but instead of sending a cheque for £48 000 he sent one for £38 400 only. He later claimed that he had made a mistake and sent off the rest a couple of weeks later, but the supplier was very annoyed and warned him against doing it again.

Self-check

How much money was in the bank at the end of this particular month (assuming a balance of nothing at the start)?

In the first situation Uncle Percy received cash from the sale of the eight cars only and he would receive the money for the other two at a later date. So, at a selling price of £5000, the actual amount of money that came in during the month was £40 000, and £48 000 went out, leaving Uncle Percy with an overdraft at the bank of £8000. The profit was £2000 because all ten cars were sold – the fact that only eight were paid for is irrelevant as far as profit is concerned.

In the second situation, because all ten cars were sold for cash, the amount of money flowing into the business was £50 000 but the sum of money going out was only £38 400. So Uncle Percy ended up with £11 600 in the bank, a fact that pleased the bank manager, but infuriated the supplier.

We have now looked at three different ways in which money and profit differ. There are many more and we will see them later. For now, the important thing to remember is that the story of a company's activities may be described in terms of the flow of money in and out of the firm or in terms of its trading activities, i.e. sales, cost of sales and profit.

1.5 What is the Business Worth?

Uncle Percy was always very interested in the results of his efforts, as shown by the profit and loss statement and the flow of funds statement, but there was always one other question in his mind at the end of every trading period, namely: 'How much is the business worth?'It is a simple question but can be very hard to answer, as we will see. Luckily there is a fairly simple starting point – all we need to do is make a list of everything in the firm that has some value, then put a value on them and add up the list.

It is very easy to list the things of value in Uncle Percy's business at the end of a trading period because he has a simple business. For instance, if he starts the month with no money and sells all ten cars during the month for cash, the only thing of value he has at the end of the month, after the bill to the supplier has been paid, is money amounting to £2000. So we could say that the business has a value of £2000.

If, however, he had only managed to sell nine cars during the month he would have ended up with no money at all (by selling only nine cars, Uncle Percy would end the month by being £3000 in the red). But he would at least have one car in his possession that he had not been able to sell. Assuming that the car was still saleable, it would be something of value in the business, and all we need to do is to put a value on it. How much should we say it is worth? You may decide that the unsold car is worth £5000 because that is how much it can be sold for. However most accountants would err on the side of caution and value the car at its cost, namely £4800. We will look at the problem of valuation of unsold items later – it is a very important subject. The technical term for unsold items is 'stocks'. So it appears that in this situation the things of value in the business add up to £4800, all in the form of stocks.

Self-check

On p. 7 you looked at a situation where Uncle Percy sold all ten cars, but two were sold not for cash but on credit. At the end of the month there was an overdraft at the bank of £8000. Was there anything in the business of value at the end of the month?

In this case the business ended up in the red, but at least Uncle Percy had a promise from two of his customers that they would pay later for the cars they had bought. Each owed the firm £5000 so although there is only a bit of paper with a 'promise to pay' statement written on it, it still counts as a thing of value. At the end of this particular month the total amount of money outstanding in this way was £10 000 – being the price of two cars sold but not paid for. The technical term for money outstanding from a sale is a 'debtor'.

We also looked at a situation on p. 7 where the ten cars were sold for cash but only eight were paid for by Uncle Percy. At the end of that particular month there were no cars in the yard – they had all been sold – and there were no debtors – all the customers had paid for their cars with cash. So the only thing of value in the business was £11 600 in cash.

So far we have been able to identify three different categories of things of value that might have appeared in a business. Naturally there are many more in real firms, as we shall see in the next chapter. For now it is enough to know that these things of value are usually called collectively 'assets' and that there are many different kinds of assets. Another thing that is worth noting is that the total value of the assets in the examples we have been looking at differs quite a lot from case to case. To save you looking back they are set out below in a table:

Example	*Situation*	*Asset type*	*Value*
1	10 cars sold for cash and paid for	Cash	£2 000
2	9 cars sold for cash; 10 paid for	Stocks	£4 800
3	10 cars sold; cash taken for 9 only	Debtors	£5 000
4	10 cars sold for cash; only 8 paid for	Cash	£11 600

These examples show that although the amount of business done was very similar, each example ended up with a very different asset value total, the differences reflecting the financial management of the firm rather than its trading skills.

1.6 **Where Did the Money Come From?**

It is one thing to list all the assets of a business and value them to come up with a total 'value of the firm' figure, but it is quite another thing to be able to prove that the total value figure is correct. Accountancy systems all over the world are designed to ensure that the value of a business is a fair one. We need not go into the mechanics of accountancy here, fortunately there is a simpler way of proving that our valuation is correct. All we need to do is ask the question: 'Where did the money come from to buy all the assets that are shown to be in the business?' Going back to the four examples above we can identify the assets in each case and try to work out the sources of the money that paid for them.

In the first example, the assets are valued at £2000 (all in cash); where did the money come from? If you look back you will find that a profit of £2000 was made on the sale of ten cars – and that alone is the source of the money.

Turning to the second situation, Uncle Percy only managed there to sell nine cars so he was left with one car in stock which we valued at £4800. Where did the money come from to buy this car? (After all the supplier was paid for them.) Going over this particular case again the following key facts emerge:

- nine cars were sold at a profit of £1800;
- a total of £45 000 came in from the sales of cars;
- a cheque for £48 000 was sent to the suppliers;
- as a result, the firm ended up £3000 in the red.

The £4800 can be accounted for (to use the language of accountants) first of all because a profit of £1800 was made and secondly because £3000 was borrowed from the bank. These two items together add up to £4800 and are the sources of money in this case. In both cases a profit of £2000 was made and this was the source of some of the money. In example 3, the remaining £3000 was borrowed from the bank, but in example 4 there is no bank borrowing at all. Instead, Uncle Percy did not pay all his bill to the supplier. He got money in from his customers, put it in the bank and did not bother to pay for all the cars he had already sold! It seems like a good idea if you can get away with it. The technical term for not paying what you owe is a 'creditor'. Therefore the £11 600 of assets was paid for with profits of £2000 and with creditors of £9600.

1.7 The Big Balance

Various words are used by accountants to describe the different sources of money that are used to pay for assets. The most common are 'capital' and 'liabilities' and it is normal to show both the assets and the capital items on the same statement. Here are the four examples we have used, set out as an accountant would do it:

Example 1

Capital liabilities		*Assets*	
Profit and loss	£2 000	Cash in hand	£2 000
Total	£2 000	Total	£2 000

Example 2

Profit and loss	£1 800	Stock of cars (1 @ £4800)	£4 800
Bank overdraft	£3 000	Cash in hand	—
Total	£4 800	Total	£4 800

Example 3

Profit and loss	£2 000	Stock of cars	—
Bank overdraft	£3 000	Debtors (1 car sold but not paid for)	£5 000
		Cash in hand	—
Total	£5 000	Total	£5 000

Example 4

Profit and loss	£2 000	Stock of cars	—
Bank overdraft	—	Debtors	—
Creditors (for 2 cars @ £4800)	£9 600	Cash in hand	£11 600
Total	£11 600	Total	£11 600

In every case you will have noticed that the total on both sides adds up to the same amount. In accountants' language the two sides 'balance', and the whole statement is known as a 'balance sheet'.

1.8 The Balance Sheet – a Working Definition

The balance sheet is a statement showing the tthings of value in a business at a point in time, together with the sources of the money to buy them. Logically, therefore, the two sides must always add up to the same amount or, in other words, they must balance.

1.9 Summary

This chapter has covered the following points:

- the meaning of profit;
- the difference between profit and money;
- the three key accounting statements – profit and loss, source and use of funds, balance sheet;
- how the three statements are related;
- what assets are;
- what capital and liabilities are.

The only other thing you need to know at this stage is that real accounts are often set out in different ways, and that accountants use different words to describe the same things.

2 The Balance Sheet (1) – Assets

In the last chapter you will recall that a key question to ask about any business is 'What is it worth?' A good starting point in an attempt to answer this question is to make a list of all the things of value in a firm, place a value on the items and then get a total value. The things of value in a business are called 'assets' and they are always included in the balance sheet if they are owned by the business.

2.1 A Case for Consideration

When Wilbur Force left the army he decided to start his own business. He had been a thrifty man all his life and his savings, together with his gratuity from the army, were enough to get started. He had always been interested in machines and mechanical gadgets and he had developed, over the years, a machine that turned old car tyres into flower tubs and barrels. Once the tub was painted it looked very attractive filled with flowers, and he had built up a modest trade in these objects as a sideline.

One of the first decisions he took was that he would buy everything the business needed and would rent nothing, hire nothing, borrow nothing. So as soon as he had taken all the necessary legal steps and opened up a bank account in the name of the firm, he set about acquiring all the things he needed to start in business.

Obviously, at the very beginning of this business the only asset on the balance sheet was the money that Wilbur had put into the bank. It was this money that he was going to use to buy all the other things to start the business.

Before he could make any flower tubs he would need a number of items; here are the main ones, with explanatory notes:

Land It is surprising how often people forget this – but if you are going to own a building then you need some land to put your building on! You also need land to park any cars and vans that you have, for visitors and deliveries. Some business organizations like to have gardens and lawns around the buildings and others will have sports fields too.

Buildings Few firms can operate without a building of one sort or another. Most firms have a number of different types of building, used for different things. Typically there will be offices, stores, workshops, garages.

Boilers Along with a building it is normal to have a boiler installed to provide hot water, possibly to be used in the production process for cleaning machinery and for staff washrooms. The boiler will also be used for central heating in winter. It is usual to refer to boilers, fixed radiators and other items of equipment that cannot be moved (such as lifts, cranes, smoke extractors) as 'plant'.

Machinery and equipment Some firms need a great deal of expensive machinery and equipment in order to operate at all. Other companies need only a little. We are not sure what kind of machinery Wilbur would need to buy, apart from the machine he invented himself. However, he may want to have a machine that paints the tubs or one that puts the tubs into boxes, and there will be many other items too – such as fork-lift trucks to carry heavy loads.

Office furniture and equipment Fitting out offices can be very expensive because, not only are there such things as desks, chairs and filing cabinets to obtain, but the list will also include typewriters and computers.

Raw materials Naturally before a product can be sold, it has to be made and, before it can be made, the materials have to be bought. Stocks of materials, as they are known, are to be found in all manufacturing firms, often together with stocks of components, parts and packaging materials. Companies not dealing in goods of any kind will still have some kind of stocks, even if it is only a store of paper.

Vehicles You may feel that Wilbur should buy a van for delivering his products to his customers. He may also need a car for himself and his sales people.

These are the main items which will have to be obtained before trading can start. There is, however, one additional asset to obtain: *people*.

2.2 People – the Human Asset

People are the most important asset in any organization – without them nothing would happen at all. There is a problem however. Although they are an asset, and are of considerable value to an organization, people are not bought by companies; they are hired. So it is very difficult to place a value on the people employed by a company. The only exception to this is in professional sport, particularly football, where players are bought and sold by the clubs just like any other asset.

There is a body of opinion that believes the balance sheet should include people as an asset item, while others think that valuation of people should be outside the accounts and form part of a 'human resource audit'. Generally, the only reference to people you will find in company accounts is the total cost of the workforce. We will look at this again when we move onto the profit and loss accounts.

2.3 The Money Drain

So far we have been looking at the assets needed to start the organization. Obviously, as assets are bought, so the original asset 'money' will become smaller and smaller. It is easy to see how it is possible to run out of cash before any trading takes place. Unfortunately the problem does not end there.

Wilbur bought his land and a nice building to house the office and the stores, and for making the tubs and barrels. He spent a lot more money on machines, vans, office equipment and supplies, and then went out and bought a load of old tyres for conversion. He hired and trained a workforce, and started to produce. This was the point at which it dawned on him that his precious cash reserves were likely to disappear altogether.

The problem, in a nutshell, was that he had to continue to spend money to make the products to sell. He could not possibly ask for the money before the customers had seen the goods – in fact there are only a few types of business that ask for money before they deliver the goods. (Possibly the best example is the holiday trade where you have to pay for your holiday before you travel.)

Wilbur had an involved production process and it took several days to turn the old tyres into tubs and barrels, packaged and ready for sale. Wages and other costs that were being incurred in making the goods were going into the products themselves so that, at any time, there was a heap of partly finished goods in the workshop. Accountants call this type of asset 'work in progress' and worry a great deal about it because a lot of money can go into it, but it is of little value unless the goods are suitable for sale. Work in progress ties up money!

Typical examples of firms with high levels of work in progress are in the engineering industries, especially heavy engineering, ship-building and aircraft being two such. At the opposite end of the scale, industries that have little or no work in progress include food manufacture and any other where it takes only a short time to turn the raw materials into a finished state.

This last point gives another clue as to why Wilbur might have a cash problem. Even when the goods are ready for sale it may be several days, or even weeks, before they are actually sold. All this time the money spent in manufacture and possibly the cost of storage cannot be recovered. Accountants refer to this type of asset as a 'stock of finished goods'.

Some trades and industries have considerable amounts of money tied up in finished goods stocks, whereas others have little or no money in this form of asset. Sometimes a policy decision by the management of the firm determines the level of finished goods stocks. For instance, a firm may decide to manufacture in anticipation of demand, by making the goods and hoping that they can be sold. Others will decide to manufacture the product only when an order has been received. The first type of policy leads to high levels of finished goods stocks; the second type of firm will only have a very small amount of finished goods in store at any one time.

Many industries that make a range of standard products do so 'to stock in anticipation of demand' as the jargon has it. They include most of the goods that we buy in the shops, as well as goods you see advertised. Shipbuilding is an example of an industry which makes to customers' order. One type of business where you are unlikely to find much in stock is the bread baker. All his output is sold on the day it is made – if he has any left at night he does not keep it for sale the next day (at least he should not do so).

You would think that, once the sale has been made, all Wilbur's problems are over. Unfortunately that is not the case. Many firms sell their goods on a 'credit' basis and this means that the cash from the sale does not come in until several days, weeks or even months after the sale itself. We met this kind of asset in the last chapter, it is called a 'debtor' and again some firms have considerable amounts of money locked up, in effect, in this asset. There are a few types of business that sell everything on a cash basis and have no debtors on their balance sheets. For instance, shops, pubs and petrol stations are all fairly reluctant to sell on credit, so they are able to obtain money much faster. Once the cash has been received from the sale, of course, the balance sheet will once again show some cash in hand. This will not be for long, though, because the money will be quickly used up in more wages, materials and on all the many other expenses incurred in running a business. If there is some spare money after all the expenses have been met, the wise course of action is to invest it and in fact many real balance sheets show the item 'investments' as an asset item. The investment can be in the form of a deposit account at a bank, government securities, a stake in another firm or even some land or property not used for trading.

This is how Wilbur's business looked at the end of his first year's trading from the point of view of the assets in the firm. Take note of the form of words used – this is normal practice.

Wilbur's Tubs Ltd
Assets as at 31 December 1988

Land and buildings
Plant and machinery
Office furniture and equipment
Vehicles
Investments in other companies

Stocks of materials
Work in progress
Finished goods stocks
Debtors
Short-term investments
Cash in hand and at the bank

There are other types of asset which you will find in company accounts and which will be described later in this chapter.

Activity

Look at the list of assets set out above. You will notice that a line has been drawn across the list dividing the assets into two parts. This was done deliberately because the assets above the line are different from the assets below the line. Can you work out what is different about these two types of asset?

The group of assets in the top part of the list seem somehow to be much more substantial than the assets in the lower part. However, the most important difference is that the top set are all assets that are kept in the business: they are not quickly used up, but are intended for long-term use. In contrast, the second set of assets are for short-term use and are 'consumed' in the normal operations of the business. The technical term for the top group is 'fixed assets' – things to be kept in the business. The lower group is called 'current assets' – things to be used up by the business.

Generally the value and quantity of fixed assets in a firm does not change much from day to day. Fixed asset items stay in the business for long periods (in the case of land, for ever) and will not need to be turned into cash ever (one hopes!).

Current asset items, however, are continually changing in both size and value. As a general rule, current assets are used up within a year and, if they are not already cash, they can be turned into money within the 'normal business cycle' (the period between buying the materials and selling the finished goods).

There is one other thing to note about the list of assets. It is set out in a special way (again a convention) whereby the assets are listed in order of what accountants call 'liquidity' – simply another way of talking about the ease of converting an asset to cash. Some assets are very 'liquid' (cash is obviously so); but others are not at all liquid.

Self-check

Which types of asset (fixed or current) are the most liquid?

The current assets in a business are more easily converted to money than the fixed assets (at least usually). The interesting thing is that, sometimes, a distinction is made within current assets themselves between assets that can be quickly converted to money and the rest. These assets are known as 'liquid assets' or 'quick assets'. The items usually included are: cash in hand and at the bank, debtors, marketable investments (or short-term investments that can easily be sold).

If you feel you need to go over what you have been reading about in this chapter, now is a good time to do it.

2.4 Some Other Assets

The list of asset items that we have been looking at covers most of the assets you are likely to find in a modern balance sheet. However, other asset items turn up from time to time, depending on the industry or the policies of the company itself. There is not enough space here to mention even a few of the oddities that occur in different industries, but here are some of the 'other' assets that can crop up anywhere.

Prepayments

Have you ever had to pay for something before you received the goods or service you were buying? Rent is often payable in advance, as are rates. Whenever a payment is made beforehand, it is included with current assets as a 'prepayment' and normally you will find the item lumped in with debtors, forming a single amount.

Goodwill

There is a lot of misunderstanding about goodwill in company accounts and it is important to know where it comes from and how it is valued. Goodwill is best illustrated by the case of Len's Launderettes.

Len owned a launderette which was quite successful. One day, he was offered another launderette (called Soapywasheteria) for £40 000. He decided to look more closely at the business and asked to 'see the books'.

The value of the assets on the latest balance sheet was only £24 000 and it was explained to Len that the extra £16 000 was goodwill. Len agreed to the deal and, in effect, paid the owner of Soapywasheteria £16 000 over the real value of the business as a kind of compensation for giving up the prospects of profit in the future. Equally Len paid 'over the odds' so that he could buy the prospect of future profits. Immediately after the sale Len's assets went up by £40 000, of which £16 000 was goodwill.

Len's accountant suggested that the item should be made to disappear as soon as possible (he actually said: 'Goodwill should be written off this year'), so that the enlarged business had a more realistic asset value.

Therefore the main points to remember about goodwill are:

- Goodwill is the excess of purchase price over the valuation of a business on the date of acquisition.
- The amount of goodwill depends on the prospects for the business and how keen the buyer is.
- Goodwill is an 'intangible asset'; it is worth having but it cannot be turned into money. So, in a sense, it has worth but no value.
- Often goodwill is written off in the year of acquisition.
- Soon, to fall into line with the practice in many other countries, British firms will have to show the value of goodwill in the balance sheet and write the amount off over a number of years.

Patents and trademarks

Patents and trademarks are also intangible assets. Firms which invent products or machines can have their invention protected from direct competition by the issue of a legal document called a patent. If another company wants to obtain the product or machine it has to buy the patent. The cost could be treated as an asset and included in the balance sheet as a thing of value. However, nowadays, most firms would consider the cost to be just another item of expense and not an asset at all.

Trademarks are similar to patents except that they refer to symbols or names that the company wants to protect. If you wanted to buy the trademark 'Coca-Cola', for instance, it would cost you a great deal of money – and you would still end up with an intangible asset only (your accountant might want you to write it off straightaway). Recently, companies which have spent a great deal of money to acquire brand-names, have included a valuation of the 'name' in their balance sheet. Otherwise, runs the argument, the balance sheet understates the value of the acquisitions.

2.5 **What Value has an Asset?**

If I buy a small radio for £20, it has a value in money terms at that moment of £20. (I may decide that it is *worth* considerably more because of its use to me; that is another story.) The problem of the value of an object only arises after some time has elapsed because it is quite likely that its value will have changed.

Self-check

As time goes by, do you think that an asset such as a cheap radio will increase its value, or lose its value?

What happens, usually is, that ordinary, mass-produced items lose their value as time goes by. However the value of some things actually increases with the passage of time, especially if the item is very rare (like a painting by a famous artist) or made of expensive materials (like a solid silver teapot). Sometimes even everyday items can actually rise in value if they survive long enough; vintage cars are a good example of this type of item.

The difficulty is this: company accounts should express a realistic value for the assets in the firm at the balance sheet date. It is, however, very difficult to calculate exactly the value of an asset at a point in time.

Self-check

How much do you think my £20 radio will be worth (or have a value of) after I've had it for one year, three years, and five years?

If your instinctive answer to this question is: 'It all depends', you are quite right! The value of an asset depends on several factors:

- its age;
- the amount of use it has had (sometimes called wear and tear);
- whether it's obsolete (i.e. has a better model, product, or invention come along since it was bought?);

- whether there is a significant demand for the item;
- whether prices are increasing fast generally (sometimes called inflation).

About the only thing to say with any degree of certainty is that my radio will probably lose value as the years go by. So:

- After one year my radio may be worth about £15 (from £13–18 is possible).
- After three years it may be valued at about £8 (from £5–15 is possible).
- After five years it will have a value of about £2 (from 0–£8 is possible).

In other words, its value will fall at a rate which depends on various factors and this leads us on to two very important words in the accountancy dictionary:

- the loss of value of an asset, from whatever cause, is called 'depreciation'; or 'amortisation', in the case of an intangible asset such as goodwill.
- the increase in the value of an asset is called 'appreciation'.

My poor old battered radio lost its value over time – in other words its value was depreciated by age, by use and, probably, because it was out of date too. If there had been high inflation or an enormous demand for cheap radios its value would not have dropped so fast.

2.6 The Traditional Basis for Valuation

We will leave the questions of asset appreciation until we come to the current cost accounts statement (Chapter 7), because there is yet another accountancy convention to meet at this stage. This convention is known as 'the historic cost convention' and all it means is that the current value of the assets in the business is based on the price that was originally paid for them. Also, in calculating the value of an asset, accountants work to three very important principles or concepts. (These three concepts were set out in a document called the Second Statement of Standard Accounting Practice or SSAP2. There have been many such statements. There is a fourth concept known as 'the accruals concept' but that one does not affect us here.) These are:

1. You assume the company is not going broke. This is called 'the going concern concept'.
2. You assume that items are treated the same way each year – in other words you stick to the same system of valuation year by year. This is called 'the consistency concept'.

3 You are cautious. This is called 'the prudence concept'. Being prudent means not counting your chickens before they are hatched and only taking a profit once you have actually made the sale. Remember, the aim is to put a realistic value on the assets of the firm.

2.7 The Assets and their Valuation

Land
Land is the only fixed asset that does not lose its value, unless it gets washed away by floods or it has been used for mining or quarrying. Instead, land grows in value and, in these days of fast-rising land values, many companies show a 'revalued value' for land and not the original cost.

Activity

If a company bought a piece of land in 1960 for £50 000 which had been used for trading every since, and the area had not changed its character, how much do you think the company would be likely to value the land in the balance sheet in 1989?

a Less than £50 000.
b More than £50 000 but less than £150 000.
c Between £150 000 and £300 000.
d More than £300 000.

The answer will depend on which country you live in because the value of land rose at different rates in different countries over this period. If the land in question is in Great Britain the value is likely to have risen to well over £300 000 by now. The company could ignore all this and simply put in the original cost or any value it chooses, but it must be careful not to undervalue itself; that is dangerous and we will see why later.

Buildings
Buildings actually lose their value over time, although, from the way house prices rise, this may come as a surprise. What actually happens is that age, wear and tear, and so on all depreciate a building, but only very slowly. (Forty to fifty years is the normal time accountants consider a building will stand – they refer to it as the 'life' of the asset.) However, at the same time, buildings are appreciating in value at a much faster rate, so their actual value tends to rise. This is not the case with very old, outmoded industrial buildings in depressed areas – these lose value fast. The current practice in many companies is to revalue property from time

to time to take into consideration current values generally, but then to reduce (or 'write-down') that value to reflect the degree of depreciation.

Plant and machinery and other fixed assets
The traditional way of valuing plant, machinery and all other types of fixed asset is as follows:

- Decide how many years of 'life' the piece of equipment has.
- Take the original cost and reduce it year by year until it is at the end of its useful life.
- The value you have at the end is what the piece of equipment is worth if sold (i.e. its value as scrap or whatever you can get for it).

All this can be translated into jargon – the original cost of the asset is depreciated over its useful life down to its residual value.

We do not need to go into how these calculations are made; the important thing to know in reading a balance sheet is that the older a piece of machinery is, the smaller will be its value. The other thing to remember is that different types of equipment have different lengths of life. A van is 'depreciated' or written down over three or four years only, whereas most industrial machinery has a life of eight to ten years – sometimes much longer.

Current assets

Stocks The traditional way of valuing stocks is with our old friend prudence in mind. Consider the case of Sam's Super Sock Shop. Apart from the fact that it was impossible to say quickly, Sam's shop had a problem at the end of the year in putting a value on the socks in stock. For example, there were five hundred pairs of red, yellow and green extra long wool socks that had been bought for £2.00 a pair. The selling price was £3.00 but recently the manufacturer had raised the cost to £2.50 with a selling price of £4.00. Also, only ten pairs had been sold in ten months. What should the value of the socks in stock be?

The prudent answer would be to value them at £2.00 a pair, since that is the cost price. The socks should not be valued at either of the two selling prices because prudence tells us not to take profit before the sale has been made, and in this case, it looks as though they will never be sold! The new cost price might seem attractive at first, but again, it is overstating the case. The only other possible valuation would be to fix a new 'sale price' – less than £2 – and use that because otherwise the socks may never be sold. The jargon expression for stock valuation in historic accounts is 'valued at the lower of cost or net realisable value'.

Debtors Debtors are money outstanding from customers and so need very little valuation adjustment except for one thing. Sometimes a business makes a sale on credit and then finds the customer either disappears or will not pay. In this case the prudent firm will call the debtor a 'doubtful debt' and ignore it in the asset valuation.

2.8 Summary

All business organizations need assets – even if it is only cash in the bank. As we have seen it is possible to have many different types of asset and it seems a good idea to have plenty of assets because they form the basis of the business; without them it would be impossible to operate. However, tying up a lot of money in assets has one disadvantage – your trading efforts may not be a success and your assets will lie idle. This is called 'commercial risk' – investing money in a business and hoping that (at least) you obtain your money back with interest.

In this chapter we have begun to look at the technical terms of accountancy and at some of the special words used, often to describe fairly simple ideas or items in the firm. Here is a list of the main points; if you are uncertain about the meaning of any term go back to the page given and check up on that term before going on.

Plant (p. 14)
Stocks (p. 15)
The human asset (p. 14)
Work in progress (p. 15)
Finished goods stocks (p. 24)
Debtors (p. 16)
Current assets (p. 17)
Fixed assets (p. 17)
Liquidity (p. 18)
Quick assets (p. 18)
Prepayments (p. 18)
Goodwill (p. 19)
Intangible assets (p. 19)
Depreciation (p. 21)
Appreciation (p. 21)
Prudence (p. 22)
Asset life (p. 22)

3 The Balance Sheet (2) – Capital and Liabilities

In this chapter you will be able to find out about the 'other side' of the balance sheet. The last chapter was all about assets – things of value in the business – this chapter will focus on where the money has come from to pay for the assets. You will then be able to name the major sources of finance and classify them.

In the last chapter you read about Wilbur's Tubs Ltd and how he decided to buy everything for the business out of his own money. He acquired many different assets and spent a lot of money before trading could actually start. Even then, it was quite a time before any cash actually came into the business. Wilbur's business was a 'one man band' at first; he set it up by himself and only used his own money to get started. This kind of firm is called a 'sole trader'.

Suppose Wilbur had started out with £50 000, the worst thing that could happen to his business within a year is either to have the business destroyed by a fire or an earthquake and not have any insurance, or to be such a poor businessman that nobody buys the goods in the warehouse. Either way he would have lost his money. In contrast, the best thing that could happen would be that the product sells like hot cakes and a handsome profit is made; or alternatively, a large company buys up the firm for £1 million (highly unlikely). These are extreme possible results of the venture – obviously Wilbur's business could end up anywhere between these positions, partly depending on luck and partly on his business management skills. The outcome is not certain; in some ways it is like a horse race – the money is staked out at the start and then you wait for the result to tell you if you won or lost. Business, especially in the early days, is all about taking a chance – the word that is used most commonly is 'risk' and the words that are used to describe the money that the owner of the business puts in himself are 'risk capital' or 'venture capital'. Very often the accounts of sole traders refer to this money simply as '*capital*'.

Activity

In addition to putting his own money into the business, Wilbur could have obtained finance from other sources. Can you think of three different sources he might have approached for more money?

There are many different answers to this question, but your choice will be included somewhere in this general list:

Other sources of money

1 Friends and relations.
2 Banks.
3 Insurance companies and other organizations that have money (e.g. pension funds, large firms).
4 Government departments; local authorities.
5 Suppliers.
6 Customers.

Let us have a closer look at each of these sources in turn.

3.1 Money from Individuals

There are three ways a business can obtain money from individuals – whether they are relatives, friends or others:

- as a gift;
- as a loan;
- as a part stake in the firm.

For a business to receive a gift from an individual is very rare and for our purposes can be ignored – you will not normally see it in company accounts.

Loans from individuals are more common, both for very small firms that are just starting up and for big companies that have been in existence for years. With very small firms, loans are often from relatives – Auntie Flo may have a few hundred pounds in the bank doing nothing in particular. If she is offered enough inducement she may take it out of the bank and lend it to the business.

Loans – the three important conditions

Auntie Flo might be induced to lend her money as long as she is satisfied about three features of the loan; she would ask three key questions:

1 How long is the loan going to be? She may only be prepared to lend her money for a year or two, or for many years, but there will be a definite date for the repayment of the loan.

2 What rate of interest will I get? She will only take her money out of the bank if the rate of interest offered is better than she is already receiving (especially if the money is going to be tied up for a long time).
3 Is there any guarantee that my money will be safe? There can be no absolute guarantee that the money will be safe in a risk business. However, often a loan is made to a business with the guarantee that an asset (worth the same amount as the loan) 'belongs' to the lender. This is called 'security' for the loan and the majority of loans to companies great and small are called 'secured loans'.

These three conditions apply to all loans and are important points to look out for in the accounts of companies. Here are the key words to remember:

- Time.
- Interest.
- Security.

There are many different kinds of loan with many names – we will look at the main ones later in the chapter.

More risk capital
Auntie Flo may decide that she would like to have a stake in the business itself. Perhaps she wants to be involved with the actual operations of the firm or is quite prepared to take a chance on a risky venture with a possibility of making a lot of money (or losing it). Whatever the reason, if she decides to invest in the business in this way, she is putting in what we have already discussed – risk capital. This brings us nicely to another important word in company acounts – Auntie has decided to share some of the risk with the owner of the company – she will share its success and its failure alongside the founder. This kind of money is often referred to as 'share capital'.

Self-check

In the last section we looked at three features that apply to all loans. Which of the three conditions do you think apply to share capital (or risk capital – the same thing)? Ask again the three key questions, substituting the word 'investment' for the word 'loan' in the first question.

The characteristics of share (or risk) capital are very different from loans and none of the features of loans apply to share capital. The answer to the first question, '*How long is the investment for*?', is 'For ever, unless you can persuade someone to buy your share from you'. The second question, '*What rate of interest will I get*?', has the answer 'It all depends on how well we trade – you may get nothing!' The third factor, relating to guarantees, does not apply at all. If you risk your money in any venture there can be no security – you are taking a chance and must be willing, if the worst comes to the worst, to lose all of it.

3.2 Money from banks

Banks usually only lend money to companies – although in some countries (e.g. Japan) it is common for banks to invest in share capital. A bank loan will have to be secured against an asset, it will be for a specified length of time and the bank will state the rate of interest that the firm has to pay. The two types of bank loan are:

- an *overdraft*, which is really a way of helping the company keep on paying its normal bills even if there is very little coming into the firm:
- a *medium-term loan*, which is used to pay for a specific asset, like a new machine.

The distinction will be clearer if we use a simple example. If you owned a small hotel at a holiday resort, all your business would be done in the holiday season – about three or four months of the year. The rest of the time no money comes in: it just goes out. If you wanted to build an extension to the hotel, you would be able to get a loan from the bank at a fixed rate of interest, and repayable by a certain date two or three years after. (This is the 'medium term'; the long term is usually more than seven years.)

If, however, you wanted to paint the outside of the hotel just before the season started it is quite likely that you would be a bit short of cash. In this case you would arrange a bank overdraft and as soon as the first guests paid their bills the money received would go to pay off the loan. An overdraft is a short-term loan because it has to be paid off within a year.

3.3 Money from Insurance Companies and Other Organizations

There are many organizations that can provide finance for companies; they are collectively called 'financial institutions' and include banks. Insurance companies, in particular, lend money to firms and often the loans are of a long-term nature. The security for such loans is usually property and the technical term given is a 'mortgage'.

3.4 Money from Government Departments

Sometimes it is possible to get money from a government department at the national or local level. There are also special agencies with funds for special purposes. If, for instance, you wanted to set up a small factory in an area of very high unemployment it is likely that there will be an organization already there waiting to provide funds for good prospects. This type of finance is sometimes in the form of loans on favourable terms, and sometimes it is in the form of a grant (imagine a government actually giving money away). It is rare to see a reference to a grant in a company's published accounts unless the sum is substantial. This is because the way accountants deal with such items is a bit involved – if you want to find out more, the official way will be found in SSAP4 (1974). This Statement of Standard Accounting Practice is called *The Accounting Treatment of Government Grants*.

3.5 Suppliers as a Source of Finance

To say that money can be obtained from suppliers is not entirely accurate. What actually happens is that a company delays paying its bills and so has use of the money a little longer than it should have. For some types of business the use of creditors as a source of finance is a key factor in the way they operate. For example, the big retail shops all obtain goods from their suppliers on credit, put the goods on the shelves, sell them for cash and hang on to the money for a week or two. Only then are the suppliers paid.

There are, however, some problems with this way of doing business. The difficulty is that the supplier may not want to trade with a company that takes a long time to pay its bills. Small firms are particularly at risk from this. However, very big companies get away with it because the suppliers do not want to lose the business.

3.6 Finance from Customers

In the last chapter (p. 15) we mentioned the situation where you have to pay for something before you get it. Holidays, tickets for a train journey or a visit to the cinema are all examples of a firm getting its money before it 'produces' the goods. Would it surprise you to learn that in the balance sheet this item is often called 'cash received in advance'? You may also find the word 'deposit' appearing in companies where it is traditional to ask the customer for a small payment in advance of the article being delivered.

3.7 Other Sources of Finance

Once a business has got going, some other ways of obtaining money turn up. All of them are connected with the fact that the firm will by now have money coming in from sales. Most of this money goes straight out again to pay wages and bills outstanding, but if the firm has made a profit three extra items appear on the balance sheet as sources of finance. These are:

Tax due Unfortunately if a company makes a profit, tax has to be paid. Luckily it is not usually necessary to pay the tax bill immediately, so the firm uses the money in the meantime (the bill to the taxman is just the same as any other bill in this respect).

Dividends due If a profit has been made it is normal to pay the owners a dividend – which is another special word for interest paid on money put into the business as risk capital. Again firms normally do not pay out the money as soon as it is due but hang on to it for a while and use it for something more pressing.

Profits left over Most firms try to operate on the basis of trying to keep some profit in the business at the end. Obviously it is an easy way of raising money if it can be done – nobody outside the business has to be persuaded to part with their money. The term that is used these days to describe this is 'retained profit', although there are other phrases in use which we will look at later.

Now that we have looked at the main sources of finance we can make a list of them, using the words that appear in actual accounting statements:

- Share capital
- Retained profits

} = Equity capital or shareholders' funds

- Long- and medium-term loans

- Short-term loans
- Deposits from customers
- Creditors
- Tax due
- Bank overdraft
- Dividends

} Borrowed capital or liabilities

The list has been divided into two parts. The top two items are called equity capital or shareholders' funds because they belong to the shareholders. The share capital is the money put into the business by the owners with the retained profits being money that the owners could have taken out of the firm but have chosen to leave in for the time being.

The rest of the list has been called borrowed capital or liabilities. The word liabilities is a difficult one; strictly speaking it means 'the financial obligations of the business' and you will find the word used in some accounts to describe every source of finance, not just borrowed money.

The thing to remember about borrowed capital is that sooner or later it has to be paid back; there is a legal obligation to do so. Equity capital, on the other hand, does not have that obligation – it is in the business as risk money and rarely gets paid back to the shareholders. Moreover, interest usually has to be paid on loans and on most other borrowings, but a company does not have to pay interest on the money invested as equity capital – a dividend is only paid if there is enough profit.

You will have noticed that a dotted line has been drawn below the item called long- and medium-term loans and the rest of the borrowed capital items. This is to show that the two types of liability are different. All the items below the dotted line have to be paid off within a year – they are all short-term loans, in effect. The technical term for these items is 'current liabilities' and you will come across the phrase time and time again.

Self-check

Individuals as well as companies have current liabilities. Which of these items is a current liability bearing in mind the definition above?

a a loan to buy a car over two years;
b your electricity bill;
c a mortgage to buy a house;
d buying a suite of furniture and paying for it over six months.

The definition of a current liability is that it has to be paid back within a year and the only items in the above list that fit that definition are the electricity bill and the buying of furniture over six months. A mortgage is a long-term loan (up to twenty-five years) and a loan to buy a car over two years is a medium-term loan.

3.8 Share Capital – a Closer Look

So far we have been looking at the capital side of the balance sheet from the point of view of a small firm just starting up. To get a complete picture of sources of finance, we need to have a look at the situation in larger established companies and one of the most important features of a big company is the number of shareholders. In the case of Wilbur's Tubs, Wilbur himself was the owner and the only shareholder. As the business grew, so the number of people putting money into the business grew. This money was share capital and the people involved were therefore shareholders; and every shareholder was a part owner of the business. This is an important point: every shareholder in a firm is a part owner of that firm and the bigger the company the more shareholders (owners) it has.

When a company first 'sells its shares' – which is the expression used to describe what a company does when it wants people to invest in it – it has to decide four things:

- How much money is needed? This is called 'share capital'.
- How many shares could it issue if it wished? This is called 'authorized share capital'.
- How many shares is it actually going to sell? This is termed 'issued shares'.
- The face value of each share. The technical term is 'nominal value' or 'par value'.

This is how it would have worked out if Wilbur's business had prospered and grown. First of all it was calculated that the firm needed an extra £4 million to be able to buy more land and to build a factory containing some very expensive equipment. It was decided to get approval to raise £5 million if that amount of money was really needed but only to ask for the £4 million there and then. It was also decided that each share to be sold would be worth 20p at face value, so that in effect the shares were being sold at the rate of five for £1. In total therefore the authorized share capital amounted to 25 million shares of 20p each and 20 million shares would be issued.

To put all this into effect a meeting had to be called of all the existing shareholders and they were asked to vote on the proposals. A meeting of this nature is legally necessary and is called an 'extraordinary general meeting of the company'. The whole affair was presented in the accounts of the company at the end of the year in this way:

Share capital

Authorized 25 000 000 ordinary shares of 20p each	£5 000 000
Issued 20 000 000 ordinary shares of 20p each	£4 000 000

It is usual to add the words 'fully paid' to this last line and if there are any shares issued but which have not been paid for, a note to that effect has to appear in the accounts too.

The words 'authorized' and 'issued' are in common use in British accounting statements but they are being replaced by two new words – authorized is being called 'allotted share capital' and issued is now being called 'called-up share capital'. The reason for these changes is that in 1981 Parliament passed the Companies Act 1981 which spells out how accounts will be presented and what has to be shown. These words 'allotted' and 'called-up' are used in the Act.

3.9 Share Prices

In the example we have been looking at, the nominal value of the shares on sale was 20p. In fact the company could have chosen any value at all as the nominal price of its shares and you will find that 5p, 10p, 25p and £1 are all quite common. In America the commonest value is $1 but many other values will be found.

The nominal or par value is not the only value that you will find in relation to shares. There are two others to know about.

Selling price

If the company issuing the shares thinks that there is going to be a big demand for the shares, the price at which they are offered for sale can be higher than the nominal value. If Wilbur's Tubs had been a popular company the selling price could have been much higher than 20p. If a price of 35p had been settled on, the company would have only needed to sell 11 428 571 shares to bring in £4 million. If they had decided to sell all 20 million shares at 35p each a total of £7 million would have been received.

The way this is handled in the accounts is to show in the balance sheet, under 'equity capital' two items:

Share capital (20 million shares at 20p)	4 000 000
Share premium account (20 million shares at 15p)	3 000 000
Total equity capital	£7 000 000

The 15p referred to is the difference between the nominal value of the shares and the actual asking price, the difference between 35p and 20p. In fact the proper definition of 'share premium' is the excess paid to a company by a member over the nominal value of the shares issued.

Activity

In the financial pages of the newspapers you will often find reference to a new issue of shares by a well-known company. Try to identify the key numbers involved, namely:

- number of shares;
- nominal value;
- asking price (sometimes called the tender price).

Market Price
If a company is big enough it can have its shares quoted on the Stock Exchange'. The Stock Exchange is a very specialized market, not selling fruit or fish but selling and buying shares in companies and also handling government's shares (usually termed stocks and bonds). If the company has its shares quoted on the Stock Exchange, a price will be named every day at which the shares in that company can be bought or sold. This is the market price and bears little relation to the nominal value of the share. For example, here are the nominal and actual prices of the shares of three famous companies:

	Nominal price	*Actual price (at 31/1/89)*
Ready Mixed Concrete (RMC)	25p	585p
Tate and Lyle	£1.00	235p
Tesco Stores	5p	159p

You will not usually find the market price of shares quoted in the annual company accounts because it changes from day to day. The financial pages of the daily papers are the best and easiest source of this information.

3.10 **Other Types of Share**

Ordinary shares will be found in every company, but in addition there are other types that can be found – here are the main ones.

Non-voting shares These are sometimes called 'A' shares and as the name suggests the owner of this type of share cannot vote at a meeting of the company in the ordinary way. These shares are entitled to dividends in the same way as ordinary shares and the only other difference is that the price of such shares is usually less than that of ordinary shares.

Preference shares This type of share entitles the holder to a fixed rate of dividend and this dividend is paid out before the ordinary shareholders get their dividend. (They get preferential treatment – hence the name.) There are several different types of preference share:

- *Cumulative preference shares*. If a company has a bad year and fails to make a profit it is obvious that no preference dividend can be paid. However, if a profit is made in the year after, the holders of cumulative preference shares get their dividend for both years at once. Again preference dividends are paid out before the ordinary shareholders.
- *Participating preference shares*. With this kind of share a fixed preference dividend is paid and then a further payout can be made if

profits are enough. The rules will state that so long as the ordinary shareholders have received a certain rate of dividend then these preference shareholders can have some more!

- *Redeemable preference shares*. This type of preference share is issued for a limited period of time only, after which the company buys them back.
- *Deferred or founders' shares*. This type of share is not all that common but is a very valuable type of share to have if you get hold of some. Holders of these shares are not entitled to dividends until all preference and ordinary shareholders have been paid. In some cases no dividend is payable for a specified number of years. Once these conditions have been satisfied, however, the holder is entitled to a substantial portion of the profits that are left – very nice if the shares are in a successful business.

The advantages of preference shares are that you have a better chance of getting a dividend and you know in advance what dividend you will get – it does not depend on how well the business has got on. On the other hand, the disadvantages are that if the company does really well and makes a good profit you do not share in that success. Also you cannot vote at the company's meetings.

3.11 A Closer Look at Loans

We have already had a look at some of the main features of loans (p. 27) and seen that there are several different sources and several different types. Here are two more important types.

Debentures

A debenture is a loan to a company at a fixed rate of interest, often for a specified period of time and often secured against the assets of the firm. Interest is payable on a debenture irrespective of whether the company has made a profit, so it is an even less risky way of investing money than preference shares. Debentures can be bought by individuals just like shares whereas many loans are negotiated direct with banks and other financial institutions.

Convertible loans

If you own what is called 'convertible loan stock' in a company, you will get interest each year at a fixed rate. At some point in time the company will offer to buy back from you the loan stock, or exchange it for an appropriate number of ordinary shares. The loan itself is often a debenture but it can be any other type of loan.

Self-check

Here is a definition of a loan to a company with some of the key words missing. Fill in the blanks and if in doubt look again at p. 27.
A loan is often taken out over a f_______ period of time; it usually carries a f_______ rate of i_______ and it is often s_______ against some of the a_______ of the business.

The missing words are: fixed, fixed, interest, secured, assets.

3.12 **Reserves**

There is just one more thing to know about this side of the balance sheet, and it is something you will find in the accounts of many British companies – the word is 'reserves'. We have seen that equity capital is made up of issued share capital, the share premium account (if any) and the profits that have been kept in the business over the years – 'retained profits'. Reserves is the word traditionally used to describe retained profits and the amount in the share premium account. (There are one or two other items that can be included in Reserves and we will discuss the main one in Chapter 6.)

A short story of greed and ignorance
A story is told of a big company that had a poor year and decided not to give a dividend to its shareholders since it had very little spare cash. One shareholder, an old lady who was very well off, wrote to the chairman and complained about the lack of a dividend. The chairman wrote back explaining the situation and he was surprised to get a very angry letter from the old lady by return of post which read: 'You cannot fool me. I've read the accounts and see that you have £3 $\frac{1}{2}$ million in your reserves. Why can't we have some of that, you misers?'

Reserves are not assets to be given out; they represent sources of finance.

3.13 **Summary**

Here is a list of all the main items on the capital and liabilities side of the balance sheet that we have looked at in this chapter. If there is a word or phrase you are not sure about check back before going on to Chapter 4.

Equity capital	*Liabilities*	
	Loans	*Current liabilities*
Authorized share capital	Debentures	Short-term loans
Issued share capital	Mortgages	Deposits from customers
Preference shares	Secured loans	Creditors
Share premium account	Convertible loans	Tax
Retained profits		Dividends
		Overdrafts

4 The Balance Sheet (3) – the Complete Picture

We can now complete our look at the balance sheet by bringing together the two sides that we have been examining in the last two chapters. You will soon be able to pick up any balance sheet and identify the main components of it, no matter how the information is presented.

If you got a hundred artists to paint a country scene on the same day and from the same spot, you would find that most of the pictures that resulted would be fairly similar, but some would be different – even peculiar. The basic content would be the same, but each artist would paint the scene in his own style and in his own preferred way.

In the same way, company accounts are pictures of the business and the balance sheet itself is a representation of a 'scene' on a particular day. The basic content of the company picture is always the same, either because it is conventional to show things that way, or because the law insists, or because it is recommended by interested professional organizations. What does differ from company to company and from country to country are the words used and the way the information is presented. You will find many ways of presenting a balance sheet – the important thing to remember is that *they all show the same information*, at least in outline, and they always have done.

4.1 A Two-Minute History

It has been discovered that the ancient Egyptians had a system of accounting related to the building of the Pyramids. Probably accounts have been kept ever since man began to trade, but they became most important with the growth and development of proper organizations. The basic accounting system we use today originated in Italy in the fourteenth century in connection with the merchants of Florence and Venice. The system, universally known as 'double-entry book-keeping', was invented for four reasons:

- to prevent fraud (or detect it!);
- to describe commercial transactions (to account for them);
- to place responsibility;
- to determine profit and decide its allocation.

The system proved so effective that in 1494 an Italian called Lucas Pacioli was provoked into writing a book on the subject. It was unfortunately written in Latin so it is not in the reading list at the end of this book.

The document called the balance sheet has been around just as long in one form or another, although there have been many modifications and changes to it since then. As a result there is no single standard layout, nor is there a universally accepted set of words. What follows is a description of the more common forms of layout you will find today and also the layouts given in the latest Companies Act.

4.2 The Traditional British Balance Sheet

Capital and liabilities	*Assets*
Equity capital	Fixed assets
and	and
Loans	current assets
and	
Current liabilites	
= Total liabilities and capital	= Total assets

The way this balance sheet is set out is sometimes called 'the horizontal method'. Remember these four things about a balance sheet:

- The totals on each side must be for the same amount of money.
- Every balance sheet represents the situation for a company at a specific moment of time.
- More often than not the asset items are listed in descending order of 'nearness' to money, and liabilities in descending order of when they have to be paid.
- If a company has any investments these are shown between fixed and current assets.

Self-check

Here is a list of a company's main asset and liability items on 31 December 1989. Set them out in balance sheet form, using the diagram and the four points set out above as your guide.

	£000
Current assets	25
Current liabilities	16
Equity capital	44
Fixed assets	40
Investment	5
Loans	10

Do the totals on each side of your balance sheet amount to £70? If they do, congratulations on getting your first balance sheet right! If they don't, then check your answer against the one set out below:

Liabilities		*Assets*	
	£000		£000
Equity capital	44	Fixed assets	40
Loans	10	Investments	5
Current liabilities	16	Current assets	25
Total	70	Total	70

4.3 The Traditional American Balance Sheet

Assets		*Liabilities*	
	$000		$000
Current assets	25	Current liabilities	16
Investments	5	Loans	10
Fixed assets	40	Equity capital	44
Total	70	Total	70

We will have a look at the actual words used in American accounting statements later (Chapter 12). For now it is enough to note two differences: the Americans set the whole thing out the opposite way to the British method, with assets on the left instead of the right. Secondly, the Americans list assets in ascending order of nearness to money, with liabilities listed the opposite way too. The content is the same, the totals are the same, it's just the presentation that is different.

Activity

This is something to do when you run short of conversation with an accountant – ask him why American balance sheets differ in their layout from British ones. (There is no real answer to this, but it's fun dreaming up possibilities.)

The American balance sheet you have just been looking at is quite common today with American companies. The traditional British balance sheet is, however, out of favour and only used in very small firms and occasionally in large companies (the banks and other financial companies use this layout most).

4.4 Traditional Layout – Vertical Methods

Here are two ways of setting out the details of the balance sheet that are common in both the British and American accounting worlds:

1		*or*	**2**	
Liabilities			*Assets*	
	£000			£000
Equity capital	44		Fixed assets	40
Loans	10		Investments	5
Current liabilities	16		Current assets	25
Total	70		Total	70
Assets			*Liabilities*	
Fixed assets	40		Equity capital	44
Investments	5		Loans	10
Current assets	25		Current liabilities	16
Total	70		Total	70

Once again the American presentation puts the items in reverse order to this within each half of the balance sheet.

4.5 Modern British Method

This layout is the most common in Britain at the present time. With the new rules about presentation first put forward in the Companies Act 1981 it remains to be seen how firms decide to set the information out from now on. There are several variations of it and the following is the most common.

Net assets employed		£000
Fixed assets		40
Investments		5
Current assets	25	
Less Current liabilities	16	
Net current assets		9
Total		54
Less loans		10
Net assets		44
Financed by		
Equity capital		44
Total		44

You will notice that there are four things about this balance sheet which makes it different from the traditional one on p. 00. The differences are:

1 Current liabilities have been shifted from the 'liabilities' half of the balance sheet and taken off the current assets instead. This has created a new item called 'net current assets'.

2 Loans have been moved from 'liabilities and are deducted from assets instead, to give another new line 'net assets'. This leaves only the equity capital on 'the other side' of the balance sheet.

3 The totals of the two halves of the balance sheet are now only £44 whereas before they were £70. This is because the current liabilities have been ignored in the 'liabilities' half and taken off the assets total as well.

4 The titles for each half of the balance sheet are different – 'assets employed' is a nice phrase meaning that assets of this value were used by the company during the year. But what about the word 'net'? It is simply a kind of shorthand meaning that the value of the assets of the business have been added up and their total value has been reduced by the amount of money owed by the business.'Financed by' is another nice expression meaning 'where the money came from to buy the assets'.

Net Assets

The balance sheet we have just been looking at is a popular way of setting out the state of affairs of companies in Britain. The reason for changing to this kind of format is all tied up with another important business problem area 'working capital' which means the financial resources available to a company for its day-to-day operations. It is usually defined as *current assets less current liabilities* or 'net current assets'.

A case to consider

On 1 March, Sam (of Sam's Super Sock Shop fame) was considering his financial position. He owed £2000 to the taxman which had to be paid during the month. He owed £300 to the electricity board and £500 to one of his suppliers. He knew he was going to have to pay all these bills in the near future and he also had to find another £1200 to be able to pay his staff their wages. He looked at his available resources: £1500 was owed him by customers – he thought he could get that in during the month. He had £800 in the bank and goods worth £800 in stock, valued at cost, which he hoped to sell in the month for £1500 – all for cash.

Sam decided to go to the bank and ask for an overdraft. What amount of money do you think he will need to tide him over – assuming no unforeseen events occur?

The way to look at a problem like this is to set out the facts first. In this case the important facts relate to Sam's working capital position, and on the first day of March, it looks like this:

Current assets	
Stocks at cost	800
Debtors	1 500
Cash	800
Total	£3 100
Less	
Current liabilities	
Tax due	2 000
	800
Creditors	
Total	£2 800
Net current assets	£300

On top of these committed expenses, Sam has to pay out £1200 in wages during the month and he ought to buy in more goods to put in stock for sale next month (say £800). So he needs an extra £2000, but has only £300 of working capital in hand. If he succeeds in selling all his stock for £1500 as planned, he will still finish up £1000 short by the end of the month. This can be proved by looking at a forecast cash flow statement for the month:

Inflows of money		
Debtors paying their bills	1 500	
Sales for cash	1 500	
Receipts	£3 000	
Outflows		
Tax	2 000	
Creditors paid off	800	
Payments for more goods	800	
Wages	1 200	
Payments	£4 800	
Excess of payments over receipts		1 800
Less Cash in the bank at the start		800
Expected cash shortage		£1 000

These figures are only estimates and, if he was unlucky, Sam could find himself as much as £2500 or even £3000 short. On the other hand, if all the money came in as expected and he did not pay for the new supplies he would only need a few hundred pounds. This example shows the importance of working capital to a business and that is why it is highlighted in the balance sheet these days; it shows the ability of the company to pay off its current debts, i.e. what it owes.

4.6 The Companies Act 1985 Balance Sheets

One of the effects of being a member of the Common Market (the European Economic Community) is that the law relating to companies should be the same across the member states of the Community. This is known as 'harmonization' and the Companies Act 1985 includes a section on the presentation of company accounts, hopefully so that every company within the Community will present accounts in a similar way. The Act actually spells out two alternative ways of presenting the balance sheet – these are referred to as 'formats' and are much more detailed than anything so far. The outline of the two formats is set out below and the complete list, as set out in the Appendix.

Format 1

		£000
Fixed assets (includes investments)		45
Current assets	25	
Creditors:		
amounts falling due within one year	16	
Net current assets (liabilities)		9
Total assets less current liabilities		54
Creditors:		
amounts falling due after more than one year		10
		44
Capital and reserves		44

Once again the content is the same but the format and some of the words are different. The important changes in words are: current liabilities become 'creditors: amounts falling due within one year', loans become 'creditors: amounts falling due after more than one year', and equity capital is now called 'capital and reserves'.

Format 2

	£000
Assets	
Fixed assets (includes investments)	45
Current assets	25
Total	70
Liabilities	
Capital and reserves	44
Creditors	26
Total	70

Does this format remind you of any other format? It is virtually the same as the traditional layout, except that all forms of borrowed money are grouped together under the one title 'creditors'. It is still necessary to distinguish between those items payable within a year and those payable after one year.

On pp. 126–7 you will find a copy of a real balance sheet, which you will see relates to the situation on 2 January 1988 for United Biscuits (Holdings) plc. The layout corresponds with Format 1 of the Companies

Act 1985, so the main headings are recognisable. However, there are one or two items you have not come across before and these are commented on below:

- **Consolidated**. This word informs us that this balance sheet refers to all the companies owned by the firm called United Biscuits. On pp. 130–1 the balance sheet for the 'Parent Company' only is shown. It is usual to focus on the consolidated figures, which are sometimes referred to as 'Group'.
- **Notes**. Rather than put all the detail into one long list, it is usual to have the details in the form of notes, on subsequent pages of the accounts. The more important ones are referred to in Chapter 8.
- **Year**. You will notice that as well as the figures for the latest year, the previous year's figures are shown. This is a legal requirement and essential for analysis.
- **Provisions for liabilities and charges**. These are sums that the firm believes it may have to pay out at some date in the future but is not certain when. A good example of prudence!
- **Tangible assets**. These are assets with a physical identity, compared with the intangible assets we discussed in Chapter 2.
- **Revaluation, etc., reserve**. At the top of the balance sheet you can see that the value of tangible assets was £557.2 million. The notes indicate that land and buildings have been revalued by over £15 million. This is assumed to be part of the equity capital of the business.
- **Minority interests**. A small amount, but occurs in many firms when a takeover has occurred. Not all the shareholders in the firm that has been bought have sold their shares to the new owners.
- **Capital and reserves**. This is sometimes called 'the shareholders' funds'. The sum of £490.5 million is the equity capital of the company as at 2 January 1988. If all the assets of the firm were sold as a going concern and all the debts paid off, this is the sum of money that would be left for all the shareholders to share out amongst themselves. It represents the 'net worth' of the company.

4.7 Summary

The important things to remember about balance sheets are:

- they represent the financial position of a firm at a given point in time;
- they show the value of assets owned by the company, its debts and its 'net worth';
- there are many different ways of presenting the information.

If you want to be sure you have mastered the balance sheet, rework the United Biscuits balance sheet in the style of Format 2 (p. 45). Remember that the two sides must add up to the same amount of money!

5 The Profit and Loss Account

The profit and loss account is as important a document as the balance sheet. Indeed looking at one without the other is a bit like visiting a famous city for the first time without a guide book: you will see a lot of interesting things but you are most likely to miss the real treasures and places of interest. Very early in Chapter 1 we defined profit as the difference between the value of what has been sold and the costs associated with sales. We will now look more closely at the definition and also at the way this account is set out in published accounts. You should then be able to take most profit and loss accounts and describe their main components.

A greengrocer's shop is a very interesting business because with hard work and good management it can be highly profitable, and even if it is managed badly it seems difficult to go broke.

Consider the case of P. Bean's High Class Greengrocery Stores. This is a shop with a good site in the middle of a busy shopping street and it has been established for many years. P. Bean himself died in 1950, the daughter retired five years ago to the Bahamas (for health reasons) and the grandson – William Pears – now runs the operation with his wife and with the help of some friends and students on Fridays and Saturdays. The family own the shop, but live away from it. Every weekday morning, William sets off very early in the van to the wholesale fruit and vegetable market to buy the produce he needs for that day's business. He likes to pay for the day's purchases immediately because that keeps him in the good books of the wholesalers and he gets a little extra discount on the cost of the goods he buys. William strives to maintain the high class tradition of the business by buying good quality produce and selling it at a fairly high price. In fixing his selling prices he aims to add about 40p to every £1 of goods he buys. Out of the 40p and all the other 40ps he has to pay all the expenses of the business.

A complete list would be extremely long, but here are some of them in order of their size and importance for this type of business (approximately):

1 Wages, salaries (including insurance and pensions).
2 Electricity, gas, water (sometimes referred to as heat, light and power).

3 Rates (no rent – they own the shop).
4 Van costs (petrol, tyres, repairs, licence, insurance).
5 Shop repairs and maintenance.
6 Packing materials (paper bags, etc.).
7 Postage, telephone, stationery.
8 Advertising.

There may be other items of expenditure – they are likely to be small in this sort of business and they would all be put together in the accounts as 'miscellaneous expenses'.

5.1 **Why Have Accounts?**

William has a simple accounting system and he keeps it up to date each evening after the shop closes. At the end of the year the accounting books are sent to a firm of accountants who produce a proper set of accounts from them. The accounts are used by William to understand better how the business has been getting on and to help him plan the future of the business better. This will include, from time to time, going to the bank manager with the accounts to negotiate an overdraft.

Within any company, however small, accounts are produced in considerable detail listing everything of significance. These accounts are needed for proper control of the business and tend to be seen by the working management of the firm only. It is not necessary to show all the accounting details to the shareholders or to the public generally and you will not see the level of detail on expenses that we listed on the last page.

William is very interested to see the details of the expenses that have been incurred by the business during the year, but the item he always looks at first is 'profit'.

5.2 **What Do You Mean – 'Profit'?**

The simple definition of profit that was given at the start of the chapter – 'the difference between the value of what has been sold and the costs associated with sales' – has two weaknesses:

- 'costs' is a very vague word; and
- profit itself is used loosely to describe a number of different things.

Costs – Relevant or Not?

Generally, the cost of something is the price at which it was bought. During the course of a year a company could buy many things, but the only costs that are actually included in the calculations to work out profit are the costs associated with the sales made during the year – these are the relevant costs.

You do not include in your calculation the cost of things bought for use next year nor money spent on things you will sell next year. For example, William's year-end is 31 December 1988. If he bought two tons of potatoes on 31 December and put them into his storeroom he would not consider the cost of them in calculating his profit for 1988.

Self-check

Is the following statement true or false?

If Wilbur made 100 tubs in December 1988 and only sold them in January 1989, the cost of making the tubs (materials, wages, electricity, packing, etc.) would be a cost included in the 1988 profit and loss account.

The costs in this example are not relevant to the 1988 profit figure and so the statement is false. The information would be seen in an account called a 'manufacturing' or 'production' account but these are usually for internal use only. In this illustration the costs would only become relevant when the goods are finally sold.

As you can imagine, the problem of working out exactly what costs should be included in the profit calculation and what should be excluded is a very involved exercise, especially in complex organizations with many products and many activities.

Profit Redefined
Profit is the excess of the proceeds from the sales of goods or services over *their* cost, and after deducting the expenses incurred in running the business (i.e. selling, distribution, administration, etc.).

5.3 The Profit and Loss Account – What is Shown

Until the passing of the Companies Act 1981 in Britain, the amount of information you were able to obtain from the accounts of companies was very thin indeed (unless you worked in the firm yourself). Now firms must publish much more detail about their operations, especially in relation to the profit and loss account. The Act lists four different ways of setting out the profit and loss account (called formats) and there are several pages of rules that have to be applied in preparing the accounts. The outline of the four formats is set out below; the detailed lists can be found in the Appendix. Some figures are included so you can see how the items add up.

Format 1

		£000	*Notes*
Turnover		100	Sometimes called sales
Cost of sales		60	
Gross profit (or loss)		40	A special use of the word profit
Distribution costs	10		
Administrative expenses	18		
		28	This line could be called total operating expenses
		12	This line is called trading or operating profit
Other income		3	The Act spells out five separate items here
		15	This line is called total profit or total income
Interest payable		5	
		10	This is net profit before tax
Tax on profit of ordinary activities		5	
Profit (or loss) on ordinary activities		5	
Extraordinary items		1	These can give more or less profit
Profit (or loss) for the financial year		6	

Points to Note about the Profit and Loss Account

- The format shown above is traditional, although until the 1981 Act it was not necessary to show the 'cost' items in the published accounts.
- Other income refers to such things as interest on investments, dividends from associated companies, and any other source not connected with the trading activities of the firm.
- Other income is always added to trading profit (sometimes called 'operating profit') to arrive at a total profit figure. From this figure interest is deducted – that is, all interest payments on borrowed capital (mortgages, debentures, overdrafts, etc.).
- Tax is calculated on profit *after* interest payments have been deducted.

This is an important point: the more interest a company pays out, the less tax it has to pay.

- Extraordinary items can be income or expenditure and are included as a separate item if they are sufficiently unusual. If you find a line like this in a profit and loss account you will also find a note explaining what it refers to. For example, in the accounts of United Biscuits there is an extraordinary charge of £7.9 million. The notes explain that the reason for the charge was a change in US taxation. Clearly not a normal trading cost.
- The last item on the profit and loss account 'profit for the financial year' is often referred to as 'earnings' or 'net income'. Even the expression 'profit attributable to ordinary shareholders' will be found, as will 'attributable to ordinary capital'. These all mean the same thing! The amount on the bottom line is what is left for the shareholders (if they are lucky).
- The account we have been looking at actually includes two other accounts. These are the 'manufacturing account' that was mentioned on p. 50 (i.e. turnover *less* cost of sales giving gross profit), and also the 'trading account' which is everything down to 'trading profit'. Purists call the whole account 'the trading and profit and loss account'.

Activity

In the example of Format 1 profit and loss account, look again at the descriptions alongside the numbers. If you were asked 'how much profit did this company make?' what would be your answer?

This is a trick question. If your answer was £6 000 you would be correct, but you are also correct if you had any of these figures:

- £12 000 – trading profit;
- £15 000 – total profit;
- £10 000 – net profit before tax;
- £5 000 – profit on ordinary activities; or even
- £40 000 – gross profit is a kind of profit.

So if you are told that company XYZ made a profit of £x, your answer has to be 'What do you mean "profit"?'

Point to remember
Always qualify 'profit' with the words describing the precise level you are referring to.

In the example, the net profit for the financial year is shown as £6 000. There are only two things that can be done with net profit for the year after interest and tax have been taken into account, and after allowing for extraordinary items. Either the profit is paid out to the shareholders in the form of dividends, or it is kept in the business and used to pay for new additional assets. Strictly speaking, these two items are dealt with in a separate account called 'the profit and loss appropriation account'. It looks like this:

	£000
Net profit for the financial year	6
Less dividends	2
Retained profit for the year	4

There are five points to notice about this statement:

- Often these items are included as a continuation of the profit and loss account itself.
- Some companies use the expression 'transfer to reserves' for the last line. This means that the amount of money is added to the balance sheet under the general heading 'equity capital', as we saw in Chapter 3.
- An alternative layout looks like this:

Statement of retained profits (or reserves)	£000
Retained profit at the beginning of the year	46
Net profit for the year	6
	52
Dividends	2
Retained profit at the end of the year	50

- There will always be an explanatory note giving details of the dividends paid or to be paid in the year. Often there are two dividend payments – an 'interim dividend' paid after six months' trading and the 'final dividend' which is paid after the annual general meeting. The amount of both dividends in 'pence per share' – how much is paid out on each share – is also shown.
- The proportion of net profit to dividends is entirely up to the company. All the profit can go to the shareholders, or none of it, or whatever proportion is decided. The company can even pay its shareholders a dividend out of the retained profits of previous years. This is called 'paying a dividend out of reserves' and happens when a company has made insufficient profit in a year to keep its dividend at the levels of earlier years.

Format 2 (outline)

		£000	*Notes*
Turnover		100	
Raw materials	50		
Other external charges	10		Costs of other bought out goods and services
Staff costs	18		Wages, salaries, insurance and pensions
Depreciation	6		See note below on depreciation
Other charges	4		
		88	
		12	This is trading profit
Other income		3	
		15	
Interest payable		5	
		10	Total profit

The account is the same below this point as Format 1.

Other Points

- The list of costs (amounting to £88) is a list of costs incurred during the year and may not be 'relevant costs' in working out profit for the year. An adjustment has therefore to be made to arrive at the 'cost of goods sold'. This adjustment is called 'change in stocks of finished goods and work in progress'.
- Depreciation is an odd kind of cost. (If you are uncertain about what depreciation is turn back to p. 21). If an asset has a value in the balance sheet at the beginning of the year of £250 and at the end of the year its balance sheet value is only £200 we can say that it has been depreciated by £50 during the year. As well as showing the loss of value in the balance sheet, accountants take it off the profits of the business. In a way they are recognizing that a little bit of the value of the asset has been used up in making and selling the company's products, so it is called a cost even though no money actually goes out during the year.

Point to remember

All companies have depreciation. It is a 'cost' and comes off profit. If it is not seen in the profit and loss account it will be found in a note somewhere; it has to be shown.

Self-check

It is worth spending a few minutes comparing the two ways of setting out the first part of the profit and loss account. Both formats start with turnover and end up with trading profit of £12 000. However, the way that number has been obtained seems very different. Can you explain the difference between the two formats? Do not worry if you cannot explain it at once – have a careful look then read the clue below.

Here is a clue to this problem. If we summarize the two formats they look like this:

Format 1		*Format 2*	
Turnover	100	Turnover	100
Less cost of sales	60	*Less* costs	88
Gross profit	40		
Less all other costs	28		
Trading profit	12	Trading profit	12

In a nutshell, the difference between the two formats is in the way the costs are classified. In the first format, costs are divided according to function (distribution, administration, etc.). In the second format, the costs are classified according to their type (wages, materials, etc.).

Format 3 (outline)

Charges		*Income*	£000
Cost of sales	60	Turnover	100
Distribution costs	10	Other income	3
Administrative expenses	18		
Interest payable	5	Profit on ordinary activities after tax	5
Tax on profit of ordinary activities	5	Extraordinary income	1
Profit on ordinary activities after tax	5		
Extraordinary charges	—		
Profit for financial year	6	Profit for financial year	6

Format 4 (outline)

	£000		£000
Charges		Turnover	100
Materials costs	50	Other income	3
Other external charges	10		
Staff costs	18	Profit on ordinary activities	
Depreciation	6	after tax	5
Other charges	4	Extraordinary income	1
Interest payable	5		
Tax on profit of ordinary activities	5		
Extraordinary charges	—		
		Profit for financial year	6
	98		
Profit for financial year	6		

5.4 The Profit and Loss Account – a Real Example

You will find on pp. 124–5 an example of a recently published profit and loss account relating to United Biscuits. Again the account is set out according to Format 1 on the 1985 Act and most of the descriptions have already been discussed. One or two items require clarification and these are noted below:

Trade discounts Some firms may include this item as a cost, others may simply show the 'net sales or turnover' figure.

Profit sharing Many companies give their employees a bonus at the end of the year if profits have reached a certain level.

Earnings per share This can be defined as profit divided by the number of shares issued on average throughout the year. The average number of shares was 412.2 million and the profit figure used of £98.4 million was after tax but before extraordinary items. Note 9 mentions 'earnings per share on a fully diluted basis'. Sometimes companies issue loan stock which is convertible to ordinary shares at some future date. Diluted earnings per share merely divides total earnings by the number of shares there will be when the loan stock is all converted.

5.5 **Summary**

You have now seen a real profit and loss account and know that there are other versions of it. In Chapter 8 you will learn more about the detail which companies have to reveal to the outside world. For now it is enough to know that companies do not often publish much more than they have to!

Activity

Try to define the following expressions by filling in the gaps in these sentences. If you are stuck look back over the chapter (especially pp. 51–3).

1 Gross profit is turnover less ________________ .
2 Trading or operating profit is gross profit less ________________ .
3 Total profit is operating profit plus ________________.
4 Net profit before tax is ________________ less ________________ .
5 Profit on ordinary activities is ________________ less tax.
6 Profit on ordinary activities after tax plus or minus extraordinary items equals ________________ .

The missing words are:
1 Cost of sales.
2 All other costs (or distribution, administration, others).
3 Other income
4 Total profit; interest payable.
5 Net profit before tax.
6 Profit for the financial year.

6 Source and Use of Funds Statement

The source and use of funds statement is the third very important document which is produced by companies to help to explain what has been going on in the business. This statement is not required by law, only recommended as good practice, indeed until recently very few firms bothered with it at all. The aim of this chapter is to help you understand why the statement is important and what it consists of, and to explain the significance of most of the items in these statements.

Have you every heard anyone say: 'I don't know where the money goes to'? Maybe you have said it yourself after an expensive day out, or at the end of your holidays. Very few people appear to have such tight control over their spending that they can account for every penny all of the time. If you are one of these people you are in the lucky minority; the rest of us either don't care or have to sit down at the end of the day or week and try to work out what we did with our money.

It is even more important for a company to do this kind of exercise because failure to control the money side of the business can quickly and easily lead to disaster.

6.1 A Case to Consider

Two brothers who were expert builders decided to set up their own firm. They were very successful at securing contracts because they were known to be efficient and produced quality work. Although they were not usually the lowest quotation for a job, customers came to them because they could be sure of a worry-free contract.

The brothers spent as little time as possible in the office, preferring to be out and about supervising the building work. Their business grew very quickly and in the space of four years their turnover increased to five times their first year's sales. Their profits rose more slowly over the period, but they were very surprised when their bank manager refused to let them borrow any more money. 'We've landed this huge contract,' they argued, 'and we need the money to buy materials, to hire equipment and so that we can pay the first few weeks' wages'. But the bank manager was not impressed: 'That's what you said last time and all that happened is that your overdraft kept on rising. It has to stop.' Can you imagine why the brothers are short of money even though the business is apparently profitable and growing?

There are several possibilities in answer to this question and the real reason may be a combination of them. Here are the most likely:

- The brothers were taking all the profits out of the business in dividends, so there was nothing left to spend on the next contract.
- Customers were not paying their bills quickly after the job had been completed. This is a very common problem because the firm does not want to offend the customer by pressing too hard for the money. So debts are left outstanding for months – is it any wonder the overdraft keeps rising?
- The brothers could be spending money on assets not directly connected with particular contracts. They may have bought a lorry or an excavator or acquired a piece of land for future development. All these would have drained the firm of cash.

Whatever the reason for the cash shortage the problem ultimately becomes critical when interest charges are so high that all the profits at the trading level vanish. Only a cash flow forecast can prevent a firm getting into difficulties like this, but the source and use of funds statement can show managers where the money went to (and where it came from) in the past. At least they will then know why they are in the situation in which they find themselves. The two builder brothers – and many small, young, growing firms are just like this – do not have the faintest idea why they are so short of money; the purpose of the 'funds flow' statement should be obvious in the light of their innocence.

The funds flow statement attempts to answer three questions:

- Where did the business get money from during the financial year?
- Where did the money go to during the year? Or: What was the money spent on during the year?
- What was the overall effect of all these transactions on the firm's balance sheet and financial health?

the flow of funds in
less the flow of funds out
equals additional money *or* less money
plus money at the start of the year
equals money at the end of the year.

6.2 **Sources of Finance**

Activity

Think of any established business you know about. It may be a small garage or a large supermarket chain, or a huge multinational oil company. Can you think of three different ways of bringing money into the business?

Money can come into a business during the course of a year in many different ways. Here are the main ones:

1 **From sales** This is the obvious one, but money will come in only if cash changes hands. The supermarket will get its money immediately a sale is made, but most manufacturing companies sell their products on credit as we saw in Chapter 2. In these cases no money comes in until the debt is paid.
2 **From debtors** This is a source related to the last point. It is possible for a company to have low sales in a particular year, but to receive a considerable amount of money from its previous year's debtors.
3 **From the shareholders** This is a source that companies will use only occasionally. However it is a good way of getting considerable sums into the firm, either as a new issue of shares for the first time or by offering more shares to existing shareholders. This is called a 'rights issue' of shares and in such cases the company offers its existing shareholders new shares at a 'good' price, usually offering one share at this price for every four or five already held.
4 **By selling fixed assets** A company can raise money by selling off some of its fixed assets. For example it may have a piece of machinery that it no longer wants, or a building or even an entire subsidiary business.
5 **By raising a loan** Borrowing money is an old-established way of getting hold of more money and is a lifeline for many firms.
6 **By not paying bills** You will recall what happened when Uncle Percy did not pay his bills (pp. 7, 8). The immediate effect was that he had more money than he would otherwise have had.
7 **Selling stocks of goods** This one is the hard one to understand because it does not seem any different to sales themselves. The difference is that by selling from stock a company does not have to spend money on new supplies. This saving is, in effect, an inflow of money and we will see how it works after we have had a look at the second question – where can money go to in the course of a year?

Again thinking of any established business you know about, can you name three different ways in which money can go out during the year?

A complete list would be almost impossible. Howeve
collective terms that will cover most things you are like

- **Operating expenses** All companies spend money on course of a year; the list itself will include all the items that pp. 48–9 in relation to P. Bean's shop, and in a big comp likely to be many more. Under this general heading we can the money spent on raw materials and other goods for sal in most companies this will be the single most important item of expense. Staff costs are the largest item of expense in labour-intensive industries like agriculture and mining and in some service industries like banking and insurance. For the rest, it is the cost of bought materials and goods that takes the most money out of the firm.

- **Stock-piling** It is one thing to buy goods or materials that you hope to sell fairly quickly, but if you think that their cost is going to rise or that there is going to be an upsurge in demand, you may decide to stockpile. This in effect means spending out money over and above what is really needed to carry on trading at the normal level. It is the opposite of selling stock (see item 7, p. 60).

- **Buying fixed assets** This was mentioned in relation to the problem of the two brothers who were builders. Fixed assets like land and buildings, machinery, vehicles and so on are essential if the business is to grow; they are tangible evidence of success. Buying fixed assets is therefore a normal healthy activity but if it is not controlled can cause a severe cash shortage.

- **Acquiring a new business** In buying a new business a company will be seeking to expand its size in a fairly substantial way. Obviously some fixed assets will usually be bought as part of the purchase price, but also the price will often include some stocks and an element of goodwill. Sometimes companies buy other business operations without using cash at all, using instead their own shares as 'money'. In that situation only a small amount of actual cash goes out.

- **Loan repayment** The problem with borrowing money is that it has, sooner or later, to be paid back. If a company has not been saving up for that day or cannot find a new source of borrowing, then it could be very embarrassed on the day the debt falls due for repayment.

- **Paying bills faster** Most firms take a little while to pay their bills and so always have some creditors. When a firm extends its creditors (see item 6, p. 60) money comes in. If it decided to reduce its creditors by paying the bills faster money goes out quicker.

[...]ng interest on loans Interest payments are not an operating [...]pense because they have nothing to do with the trading side of the firm. These outflows of money need to be separately identified because they are compulsory – failure to pay interest is a sign of impending collapse!

- **Paying the taxman** These outgoings are also compulsory and have a high priority in any sensible firm. Often tax is paid well after the profits have been made and company can find itself having to pay a huge tax bill in the middle of a very poor year, because the previous year was so profitable.

- **Giving customers longer to pay** If a company decides to extend the period of credit it allows its customers, it is in effect getting in its money more slowly – the same effect as an outflow of funds.

- **Paying a dividend to shareholders**.

6.3 The Funds Flow Statement – the Complete Picture

Sources (inflows)

The funds flow statement usually starts with one of the figures of profit taken from the profit and loss account. This is often 'profit on ordinary activities before tax and interest'. Profit is used rather than sales because it is helpful to be able to tie together profit and money, and also because it avoids the need to spell out operating costs as an outflow. The first line is therefore:

1 *Profit on ordinary activities (before tax and interest)*
Before adding in the other inflows we listed on p. 60, there is one very important adjustment to make to this profit figure before it can be described as an inflow of funds; the figure in the profit and loss account for depreciation has to be added back. On p. 54 we mentioned that depreciation is the accountants' way of recognizing that the value of fixed assets has been reduced over the accounting period, and profits are reduced in line with the loss of value. However depreciation is not a flow of money out of the business – it is merely an accounting adjustment and so 'profit' actually understates the amount of money flowing in. Thus the second line is:

2 *Depreciation*
The remaining inflow lines are:

3 *New share capital*

4 *New loans* (except bank overdrafts which come at the end)

5 *Proceeds from the sale of assets and businesses*

6 *Reduction in stock levels*

7 *Reduction in debtors*

8 *Increase in creditors*

} Between the beginning and end of the year

Uses (outflows)
The uses part of the statement will contain the following items:

1 *Interest payments* (this should tie in with the profit and loss figure)

2 *Taxation* (this will not be the same as in the profit and loss account)

3 *Dividends paid* (some of the dividend paid will relate to the previous year's profits)

4 *Loan repayments*

5 *Purchase of assets* (fixed)

6 *Purchase of new businesses*

7 *Increase in stocks*

8 *Increase in debtors*

9 *Reduction of creditors*

} These three are the opposite of the inflow items and relate to the difference between the beginning and end of the year.

The last three items on both the inflow and outflow lists – stocks, debtors and creditors – are called 'working capital items'. These were referred to earlier when we looked at the balance sheet (p. 43).

6.4 Funds Flow in Practice

Most companies present their Source and Application of Funds statement in accordance with the officially recommended method; this is SSAP 10. However, you will find many variations within the general framework and these can cause problems for experts as well as casual readers. In fact, some people think the present way of showing the information is very poor. If the statement you are looking at seems confusing, here's what to do:

- List all the inflows
- List all the outflows
- Deduct one from the other
- The difference will be the change in cash, short term bank deposits, loans and overdrafts

6.5 A Real Funds Flow Statement

On pp. 128–9 the funds flow statement for United Biscuits is set out. You will see that it is in line with what has been described, but has one or two interesting variations.

First, the source of funds part is divided into two, showing funds generated from operations – the ordinary trading activities of the firm – and funds from other sources – including selling off assets and issuing more shares. The second point to be noted relates to the last three lines of the statement under the heading 'Movement in net liquid funds'. The use of brackets may seem confusing; however, in the 1987 column they indicate that these sums went out of the firm. A total of £42.3 million was spent on (mainly) new assets and loan repayments, more than was generated. Bank balances, cash and deposits fell by £48.4 million as a result – the difference of £6.1 million being a reduction in overdrafts and other short-term loans. These figures can be checked by reference to the consolidated balance sheet, being the difference between the 1987 and 1986 figures.

6.6 Final Points on Funds Flow Statements

This kind of statement has been required in Great Britain only since 1975 with the publication of SSAP10. In the USA the movement began in 1971, where the statement is usually called SCFP, standing for 'statement of changes in financial position'. At this stage there is no general agreement as to how it should be set out, nor even precisely what the word 'funds' means. Each statement is designed to help explain the changes that have taken place in a company's balance sheet from one year-end to another. Some people think it is a waste of time. (see 'Let's Scrap the Funds Statement', L. C. Heath, *Journal of Accountancy*, October 1978). If you are prepared to spend a little time studying it and shifting the numbers around, it can be a very helpful document in explaining how a company has managed the money side of its affairs.

7 Current Cost Accounts Statement

The 'current cost accounts statement' is another recent innovation in the published accounts of companies. It is sometimes called 'accounting for inflation' which gives a clue as to what it is all about. Accounts prepared on the traditional basis of 'historic cost' (see p. 21) suffer from the fact that in some respects they do not adequately reflect the effect of inflation on the value of the business. This document is an attempt to remedy this deficiency. By the end of the chapter you should be able to explain the main items in this statement, and give reasons for their inclusion.

In Chapter 2 we looked briefly at the question of how assets are valued. In the profit and loss account and in balance sheets the basis of valuation is still the historic cost convention. In fact the Companies Act 1985 sets out rules for the valuation of assets, under the general heading 'historical cost accounting rules' (see Companies Act 1985, Schedule 4, Part II, Section B), which state that assets should be valued at their purchase price or production cost (less depreciation where appropriate). This sounds like a good system at first glance but as usual there are some snags.

A Case to Consider (1)

Wilbur Force decided to buy a small lorry for his business on the 1 January 1989. The lorry was going to cost him £7000 and he decided that after four years it would be a bit battered and unreliable, so he would then sell it. He guessed that he would sell it for about £600 only and he would then have to go out and buy a new one. He was worried about the fact that he would need to be able to find £6400 of extra money to get the new lorry, so he decided to save up for it by putting in the bank every month a sum of money equal to the depreciation that was being shown in his accounts. Wilbur's accountant pointed out that a sum of money equal to the amount of depreciation should always be spent on replacement fixed assets, simply to keep up the value of the business. What was more, if there was no depreciation, every time you wanted to replace an asset you would have to raise new finance from outside.

Depreciation is sometimes calculated in such a way that the amount written off is highest in the early years and less when the asset is old. This probably reflects more accurately how asset values really decline and is also not such a drain on profits when there are high repair costs in later years. The name for this system is 'reducing balance depreciation'.

Wilbur decided, therefore, to save £2880 by the end of the first year, £1580 during the second year, £870 during the third year and £470 in the fourth year. So on 1 January 1993 he would have £6400 saved up, and with the £600 from the sale of the lorry, he would be able to get a new one.

Activity

Do you think he would have enough money for a new lorry on 1 January 1993. If not, roughly how much do you think he would be short (ignoring any interest from the bank)?

A vehicle which cost £7000 in 1989 is likely to cost considerably more in 1993. It all depends which country you live in as to how much extra the lorry would cost in four years, but anything between £8500 and £9500 would be considered not abnormal during this period. So poor Wilbur is likely to be at least £1500 and possibly £2500 short of money to buy a new lorry just like his old one.

Therefore, the first reason for adjusting the accounts is to have a sufficient amount of depreciation to allow for the effects of 'inflation' – which we defined in Chapter 2 as a general increase in prices. However, as far as a company is concerned, the only inflation it needs to worry about is the increase in prices that affect it. Inflation has always been a part of business life, but it is only since the mid-1960s that there has been a common concern about it. Until then people who said that accounts should be adjusted for inflation were regarded as a bit odd. However, once levels of inflation became high many experts agreed that something should be done – many are still arguing about what should be done and how.

We do not need to mention all the arguments here; the reading list at the end of the book will help if you want to find out more. In this chapter we are going to concentrate on the ways inflation affects accounts and how accountants handle things at the moment.

A Case to Consider (2)

On p. 22 you were asked to guess how much you thought a piece of land would be worth in 1989 if it had been bought in 1960 for £50 000 and assuming that it was still a desirable piece of land to have for business purposes. It was suggested that the value in 1989 could be well into six figures – possibly even as high as £300 000. There was a company once that had bought some land in 1935 which was standing in the books at a few thousand pounds – the original cost – even in 1968. The company had been going through a lean spell for several years and the owners decided to sell up while the going was good. The price they got was the book value of the assets plus something (not a lot) for goodwill, and everyone was very surprised when the buyer immediately resold the land for redevelopment at an enormous profit. The moral is: *do not undervalue your assets; somebody else will make money out of your neglect – sometimes by an unwelcome take over bid.*

The second reason for adjusting the accounts for the effects of inflation therefore is to maintain the value of the business at a realistic present-day value.

A Case to Consider (3)

Let us consider a company that trades in nuts (the edible type). Every autumn it buys tons of nuts from all over the world, packs them into small cartons and sells them to grocery shops at a huge profit. In 1986 it bought 500 tons of nuts, sold them for £60 000 and made a profit of £9000 before tax. Its profit margin on sales was 15%.

In 1987 the company again bought 500 tons of nuts, sold these for £66 000 and made a profit of £9 900 before tax, also a profit margin of 15%.

The owner decided that he wanted more profit for less effort, so in 1988 he bought 1000 tons, stored half of them and sold the other half for £70 000 and made £10 500 profit (15% again). The next year (1989) he bought more nuts, but stored them all and simply sold all the previous year's nuts – this time his sales were £80 000 and his profit was £16 000, a profit margin on sales of 20%.

Self-check

Think about this case for a few minutes and try to work out how the owner apparently became so much more efficient. Also do you think the business was so much more efficient?

One way of describing the effect that has been created is to say that sales are made at today's prices, but most costs are at yesterday's prices. We know that yesterday's prices are less than today's prices, so the profit that has been made is artificially high. To have achieved a profit margin of 15% and been consistent, his profit in 1989 should have been £12 000 only. As it was he made £16 000, including £4000 for buying early, and that cannot really be more efficient – smarter, yes; more efficient, no.

7.1 Today's Versus Yesterday's Money

Inflation can create an illusion not only of increased efficiency but also of growth. Look at the profit record of our nut company over four years:

	Profit before tax		*Profit before tax*
1986	£9 000	1988	£10 500
1987	£9 900	1989	£16 000

The picture created is one of continuous growth. But we know that the quantity of nuts sold each year was 500 tons. All that happened in the first three years was that prices went up, and in the fourth year a change in the buying policy of the firm magnified the growth illusion.

The third reason to adjust for inflation is therefore to remove the illusion of growth and efffiency created by inflation.

The fourth reason for adjusting the records also relates to measures of efficiency, here the crucial measure of success for a business – 'profitability'. We will look at this criterion in part II; let us assume that:

trading profit ÷ total assets (in percentage form).

For example, a company with a trading profit of £5000 and total assets of £50 000 has a 10% rate of profitability, and the higher the percentage the more profitable the business.

Activity

Look at this example of a company labouring under the inflation illusion; can you say why it is not as successful in the second year as it seems?

	Year 1		*Year 2*	
	£000		£000	
Turnover	200		220	
Less costs	180		198	
	20		22	
Less depreciation	10		10	
Trading profit	10		12	
Assets	100		90	
Less depreciation	10		10	This is calculated at 10% of the original cost
Book value of assets at end	90		80	
Profitability		11.1%		15.0%

Prices and costs rose by 10% but depreciation was calculated on the historic cost basis and so was a smaller sum in the second year. This had the effect of inflating profits even further. On the other hand, the assets were included at their original cost (the day before yesterday's prices) and so the profitability calculation uses a smaller value for assets than is realistic.

The only way in which it is possible to say that the company is more efficient in the second year is that it has operated successfully with older assets and to that extent deserves some credit. If the assets were revalued at 10% as well as costs and revenue, and depreciation was calculated on that basis, the resulting figure for profitability would be about 12.5%.

7.2 **The Inflation Danger**

The real danger to a business of a high rate of inflation is that the artificially high profit figures created may tempt the directors of the firm to distribute more of that profit than is prudent. The need to be prudent in times of inflation is all the more important because more money is needed to stay in the same place. The volume of business may be the same from year to year, but this year's retained profit has to pay for next year's higher cost of purchases and the increased amount of money tied up in debtors. If too much profit was distributed, not enough money would be available to keep going at the same level of activity.

The present system of current cost accounting is designed to show the maximum amount that could be paid out (by way of dividends, and taxation and interest) without eroding (or reducing) the operating assets of the business. Another way of putting it is that the aim is to keep up the operating capacity of the business.

We have already considered the fixed asset side of the problem; the particular concern here is that the firm's working capital (stocks, debtors, creditors) may become insufficient to maintain the business at its current level.

7.3 **Current Cost Profit – the Adjustments to Make**

Company accounts until recently were required to show a 'current cost accounts' statement which is set out according to the requirements of

SSAP16 which was published in March 1980 (Statement of Standard Accounting Practice 16, *Current Cost Accounting*). Some companies still show this information, and on the current cost profit and loss account you will find four 'adjustments' that are made to the 'historic' profit figure. The calculations are fairly involved and are not included in this book; if you want to know exactly how the adjustments are made see the reading list at the end of the book.

1 Depreciation

The ordinary profit figure is reduced by an extra amount of depreciation such as we have already seen.

2 Cost of Sales

This involves revaluing goods in stock at the beginning and end of the year so that the cost of goods sold is at current cost not historical cost. The usual effect is to show a higher cost of sales figure and so a lower profit figure.

3 Monetary Working Capital

One way of looking at inflation is the effect it has on money over time. As time goes by the value of money falls, and the faster prices and costs rise, the quicker the value of money falls. The cost of sales adjustment is a way of dealing with the loss of value of money tied up in stocks. In the same way the monetary working capital adjustment is a way of dealing with the loss of value of money because it is tied up in debtors, taking into consideration creditors which help to ease the problem.

7.4 The Gearing Adjustment

The fourth adjustment to the historic cost profit figure is called the gearing adjustment. 'Gearing' is a technical term that refers to the proportion of a company's assets that are financed by equity capital or by borrowed capital. A company has a high level of gearing (or is highly geared) if it has a relatively high proportion of loans and other borrowings; whereas a firm with little debt has a low gearing.

The reason for making an adjustment in the accounts related to a company's gearing is not obvious at first. This is how the reasoning runs:

- The other adjustments make sure that the firm has enough resources left in the business to pay for the inflated costs of running it.
- In general these adjustments reduce the historic profit at the operating level, so that less dividends can be paid out.

- In effect the shareholders are being asked to pay (by giving up their dividends) for *all* the increased value of the assets.
- This is unfair, since some of the assets have been paid for with borrowed money.
- Therefore the profits should not be reduced as much as the operating adjustments indicate.
- The amount to add back depends on how highly geared the business is. A low geared company will have a small gearing adjustment; a highly geared firm has a large adjustment.

The actual calculation ignores any borrowings that were included in the monetary working capital adjustment, but does count the revalued value of assets. The actual calculation of the gearing percentage is a little different to the one we used on the last page:

net borrowings × 100 ÷ (shareholders' equity + net borrowings).

'Net borrowings' mean all borrowings except those included in monetary working capital. Shareholders' equity is share capital, retained profits, other reserves and the surplus coming from the revaluation of assets. The sum of these two items which is used for the gearing ratio is equal to 'net operating assets'.

Whatever the percentage turns out to be, it is applied to the total of the three current cost adjustments. For example, if the net borrowings were £4000 and shareholders' equity was £8000, the calculation would be:

gearing percentage = (£4000 ÷ (£4000 + £8000)) = 33.3%.

If the sum of the current cost adjustments was £6000, the gearing adjustment to add back would be 33.3% of this, i.e., £2000. This would reduce the amount of the total adjustment to £4000.

7.5 Adjustments to the Balance Sheet

As well as producing an adjusted profit figure, the balance sheet is altered in current cost accounting to reflect current values. The main adjustments are obvious from what we have been discussing in this chapter so far and they are as follows.

Assets

- Fixed assets.
- Stocks.
- Investments (included at valuation or market valuation).
- Trade debtors and trade creditors to give monetary working capital.

Many companies revalue their fixed assets fairly frequently, and the balance sheet notes will state the amount by which the assets have increased in value in the year.

Liabilities

Share capital and reserves – the total of all the revaluations is included as a separate reserve, the 'revaluation reserve' (noted already on p. 46). Also, the historic profit and loss figure is replaced by the 'retained current cost profit' figure.

Current Cost in Practice

Not many companies are nowadays showing current cost accounting information, apart from the revaluation of fixed assets already noted. United Biscuits accounts for 1987 did not include a current cost statement. Some firms produce an abridged version; J. Sainsbury plc's 1988 accounts, for example, include a statement showing that the company's profit before tax would fall from 3308.4 million to £300.2 million if current cost adjustments were made, and earnings per share would be 13.02p on a current cost basis rather than 13.63p on the historical cost basis.*

British Gas, however, presents its figures primarily in this form.**

7.6 Summary

More has been written about accounting for inflation over the last 20 years than all the other finance and accounting matters put together and the debate is by no means over. The Chartered Institute of Cost and Management Accountants has already made some proposals (May 1983) to replace SSAP16, and no doubt there will be many others. Watch the news to see what happens, but always keep in mind these points:

- Inflation makes the numbers bigger.
- A company's real value is much higher than its historic cost value.
- Companies must be prudent and retain enough profit to pay for inflated asset values.
- Profitability may look good on historic figures, but it is the current cost basis that gives the real clue to efficiency.

*See J. Sainsbury plc Annual Report 1988, p.42.
**See British Gas Annual Report 1988, pp. 20–32.

8 Value Added and Other Information

The value added statement is not compulsory – firms do not have to produce it. However where it is shown it can be a very useful source of information about a company and its activities. A government green paper published in 1977 (*The Future of Company Reports*, Cmnd 6888, HMSO, London) recommended that such a statement be shown and the accountancy profession itself suggested it in 1975 (The Corporate Report, Accounting Standards Steering Committee).

The aim of this chapter is to show the purpose of a value added statement, how it is built up and what it contains, so that you will be able to look at such a statement and comment on it.

Think again about P. Bean's High Class Greengrocery Stores (p. 48). Do you remember the way William fixed his prices? He decided that he would add 40p to every £1 of goods he bought and that would have to pay for all the expenses of the business during the year. At the end, hopefully, there would be a bit left over as profit. So if he bought something for £1.00 (say, a very large bunch of bananas), his selling price would be £1.40. Accountants refer to the 'gross profit margin' when they are dealing with this area as we saw on p. 51, and in this case the margin is 40p as a percentage of £1.40, that is 28.6% approximately. If his turnover in the year was £300 000, the gross profit would be in money (roughly) £86 000 (precisely, it is £85 800). This is the total gross profit, out of which all the expenses listed on pp. 48–9 have to be paid.

With the £85 800 of gross profit, William has to pay many other bills for outside services and goods. In fact the list on pp. 48–9 is a list of all the outside suppliers to the shop – except for wages which can be counted as 'inside costs'. Let us imagine that the total paid out to all these other suppliers was £45 800. This would be the cost of heat, light, rates, van costs, repairs, advertising, telephone, post and so on. By now he has only £40 000 left and it is this sum of money and the corresponding sums in all other companies that value added is all about.

8.1 A Working Definition

Value added is the difference between the revenues and other incomes of a company and the cost of goods and other bought-out services. (Note: the definiton of 'value added' for calculating value added tax is a different matter and is not directly related to the value added statement in company accounts.) The value added figure of £40 000 left in William's business could be used in various ways. The complete list of end uses is:

- Wages.
- Depreciation (it could be called a payment to the business to maintain asset values).
- Interest payable.
- Tax.
- Dividends to shareholders.
- Retained in the business (it could be called a payment to the business to expand the assets).

Another way of looking at value added is to consider it as the sum of all the items on that list. Crudely stated, value added is trading or operating profit *plus* staff costs *plus* depreciation. Here is an example, using different numbers; starting with the profit and loss account:

		£000
Turnover		500
Less bought materials and services	200	
Staff costs	180	
Depreciation	40	
Trading profit		420
		80
Less interest payable		10
Profit before tax		70
Taxation		30
Profit for the year		40
Dividends		30
Retained profits		10

Value added can be obtained in three ways from this example:

	£000
1 Turnover	500
Less cost of bought goods and services	200
Value added	300
2 Staff costs	180
Depreciation	40
Trading profit	80
Value added	300
3 Staff costs	180
Depreciation	40
Interest payable	10
Taxation	30
Dividends	30
Retained in the business	10
Value added	300

Sometimes value added called (surprisingly) 'added value' because it represents the amount that is added to the goods, materials and services that have been bought outside. It is a measurement of the wealth that a company has created.

If I bought 1000 tons of coffee for £5 million and sold it all for £5 million, I would have created no wealth at all. If, however, I sold the lot for £6 million then I would have created wealth of £1 million, and if I paid out £800 000 for insurance, shipping costs and all the other external costs then the value added – the wealth – would have been only £200 000.

This then is the first reason for calculating value added: it measures the wealth created by the firm, and by comparing a company's value added figure against its previous years' figures it is possible to see how fast it is growing in a real sense.

The second reason for calculating value added is tied up with the list of items given in item **3** above. Each of the six entries represents a different kind of interest in the business:

- **Staff costs** represent the workforce; all the clerks, manual workers, managers and directors, etc. Indeed everyone in the company who is paid for their services.

- **Depreciation** represents the fixed assets tied up in the company; the buildings, the equipment and the vehicles.
- **Interest** is the payment to a lender for tying up money in the firm.
- **Taxation** is the payment to the government (or to the state or nation).
- **Dividend** is the payment to the shareholders.
- **Retained profits** are for the firm itself to allow it to grow.

On top of these, turnover is related to the company's customers, and the cost of goods and services bought from outside is related to the firm's suppliers. The word used to describe all the different groups that have an interest in a business is 'stakeholder' and the value added statement identifies the payment or 'reward' to each one.

The third reason for calculating value added is that for some industries it is a very useful basis for analysis and is often used instead of the sales turnover figure.

For example, suppose I want to measure the growth of my coffee importing business. In the first year my accounts looked like this:

Roger's Coffee Imports

	Year 1
Sales	*1 000 tons*
	£000
Turnover	6 000
Cost of sales	5 000
Gross profit	1 000
Other charges	800
Value added	200
Other costs	160
Trading profit	40

If, in the second year, the cost to me of the coffee went up by 20% and I bought another 1000 tons, the cost would go up to £6 million. If no other costs went up I might simply pass on the extra cost to my customers, giving me a trading account like this:

	Year 2
Sales	*1 000 tons*
	£000
Turnover	7 000
Cost of sales	6 000
Gross profit	1 000
Other charges	800
Value added	200
Other costs	160
Trading profit	40

Self-check

By how much did the business grow from year 1 to year 2?

a 20%.
b between 10 and 20%.
c between 0 and 10%.
d zero.

In this example there are several possible measures of growth – we will have a closer look at this question in Part II of the book – but here most indicators show that there has been no growth at all (**d**), especially in the all-important 'volume sold' figure. If we had taken cost of sales as our criterion we might have come to the conclusion that growth was quite fast, and then we would have seen a constant profit figure and said: 'What an inefficient firm, a 20% increase in sales but no increase in profit.'

In most companies it is difficult to get a 'volume sold' figure and so value added is the next best thing; it helps to prevent you falling into the trap of seeing growth (or decline) when there is none. Many industries use value added in preference to turnover because their prices are fixed by the cost of the bought materials, etc. which can vary up or down for all sorts of reasons. Examples include textiles, printing, electrical contracting, building and firms using very expensive materials such as copper (e.g., cable making) and precious metals.

Value Added – an Example in Practice

A recent example of a value added statement is shown below. It is reproduced from the accounts of Marks and Spencer plc and relates to the year ending 31 March 1988. You will notice that the statement is called 'Application of Group Sales Revenue' and from it you can work out what the value added was, how it was allocated to different stakeholders, and how every £1 of sales revenue is used by the company.

8.2 Value Added – Three Points to Remember

One of the criticisms often made of value added is that it is no more than a device to make accounts have less emphasis on profit: presumably based on the idea that there is something wrong with the notion of profit.

Another criticism is that the information is there in the profit and loss account anyway, so the whole exercise is a waste of time.

The third criticism – and this has more validity – is that some may equate it with efficiency. It is not a measure of efficiency, just a measure of wealth creation. For instance, if a company had value added of £2 million and in the following year increased the figure to £3 million, that company would not be any more efficient if all the extra £1 million went out on wages. The firm was very good at wealth creation – but was not being any more efficient. It is quite possible to increase value added and have smaller profits – the firm has to decide for itself what its objectives are and then decide what its measure of success is. Value added is not a measure of profitability, as we will see in Part II.

8.3 Company Accounts – Other Information

The information that companies make available to outsiders – and that includes shareholders in this context – depends firstly on the size of the company and then on a variety of laws, regulations and recommendations. The three sources of rules as far as British companies are concerned are:

- Companies Act 1985 (which consolidates the Companies Acts of 1948, 1976, 1980 and 1981).
- Statements of Standard Accounting Practice.
- Stock Exchange (Admission of Securities to Listing) – obviously only applicable if the company wants to have its shares quoted on the stock market.

Three separate categories of people outside the company have to receive accounting information about the firm. Firstly, the tax authorities are able to ask for any information they want, but no one else sees it. Secondly, the members of a company must be given enough information for them to be able to make sensible judgements on the way the firm has been run (assuming that the owners and the management are separate

MARKS AND SPENCER PLC
APPLICATION OF GROUP SALES REVENUE

	1988 £m	% to total	1987 £m	% to total
To suppliers of merchandise and services	**3,401.9**	**68.4**	3,154.0	68.7
For the benefit of employees				
Salaries (including welfare staff)	**408.3**		388.0	
Deductions for income tax and national insurance	**89.5**		87.1	
	318.8		300.9	
Pension schemes	**49.4**		45.4	
Employees' profit sharing schemes	**12.4**		9.0	
Welfare and staff amenities – excluding related staff salaries of £9.9 million (last year £8.9 million)	**16.2**		15.6	
	396.8	**8.0**	370.9	8.1
To central and local government				
United Kingdom	**706.6**		647.2	
Overseas	**49.2**		46.8	
	755.8	**15.2**	694.0	15.1
To the providers of Group capital				
Interest on loan capital and overdrafts	**22.2**		28.6	
Income tax deducted	**1.0**		1.0	
	21.2		27.6	
Dividends to shareholders of the Company	**135.8**		119.5	
	157.0	**3.1**	147.1	3.2
For the replacement of assets and the expansion of the business				
Depreciation	**85.0**		68.8	
Deferred taxation	**(9.7)**		(1.5)	
Retained profits, after adjusting for minority interests	**187.5**		156.5	
	262.8	**5.3**	223.8	4.9
Group sales revenue, including sales taxes	**4,974.3**	**100.0**	4,589.8	100.0

and different people). This also applies to clubs and societies; if you are a member of a tennis club, for example, you should get a copy each year of the club accounts.

The third category is the world at large and the Companies Act has the rule that if a company is 'limited' then it must send its accounts to the Registrar of Companies where they can be seen by anyone who is interested. The technical words for all this are 'filing' the accounts, 'publishing' the accounts and the 'disclosure of information'. ('Limited' is short for a company with limited liability, which means that the shareholders are risking only the actual money they invested. If the firm goes broke the shareholders cannot be asked for more money.)

The Companies Act 1985 states that small companies (defined below) need not file a profit and loss account, nor some other details, and only need to file a shorter balance sheet.

Medium-sized companies can file a modified profit and loss account; they do not need to show turnover, but can start with 'gross profit' instead.

These 'filing exemptions' apply only if the company fits the following specifications:

	Turnover not more than	*Balance sheet total not more than*	*Average* number of employees not more than*
Small	*£1 400 000*	*£700 000*	*50*
Medium	*£5 750 000*	*£2 800 000*	*250*

*(Average is calculated on a weekly basis)

To qualify, a company has to satisfy any two or more of these conditions for both the year itself and the previous year (Companies Act 1985, Section 8(1).) These exemptions only apply to filing with the Registrar of Companies; the owners must still have all the information set out in the laws.

The majority of companies publish their accounts in the form of booklets which are available, by right, to the public in general as well as to the shareholders. You will find a great deal of additional information in these. Some of it is neither very interesting nor useful to the average reader, but the most important parts are described below.

Chairman's Report

The chairman's report or statement takes many forms but its aim is usually to describe what went on during the year, explain any exceptional events and take the opportunity to thank the staff for their hard work, singling out any individuals who did anything very special. At worst, a chairman's statement is a set of excuses for a bad year; at best it is an insight into the company's thinking with some indications as to its plans.

The Directors' Report

This report is legally required and has to contain certain information. One of the major items is a review of activities which gives more information about what the company has been doing. This report has also to give the names of the directors of the company, with the number of shares and debentures each holds. Two other items of interest are the amount the company gave to political organizations and to charity (where the amounts were over £200) and details on the employment and training of disabled persons. If a political donation exceeds £200 the recipient has to be named.

Five-year Record

The five-year record summarizes the key financial information of the company for five years. The information in this report is not very detailed, but often contains some interesting statistics as well as the turnover and profit data. You will find the five-year record of United Biscuits on p. 167. We will look more closely at the figures in Part II, for now have a look at the trends and try to spot the items that have risen fastest and slowest over the five years.

Auditors' Report

The auditor has a very important function in every company. Indeed every organization that has any financial transactions should be audited whether or not there is a legal need to do so. The auditor is an independent accounting expert whose job is to make sure that the accounts of the company are a fair reflection of its financial activities. The auditor examines the accounting books and then decides if what is to be presented is accurate. The auditors' report usually is set out in this form:

> *To the members of the ZYX Company*
>
> We have audited the accounts on these pages in accordance with approved auditing standards. In our opinion the accounts give a true and fair view of the state of affairs of the company at 31 December 1988 and of the profit and loss source and application of funds for the financial year ending on that date, and comply with the Companies Act 1985.
>
> London, 31 March 1989.
>
> Able, Baker, Charlie & Co.
> Chartered Accountants

If the auditor's report is set out in these terms then things are going well as far as good accounting practice is concerned. If, however, the words 'however' or 'reservation' or 'not able to determine' crop up, the auditors are not happy about something. Technically this is called 'qualifying the report' and nobody treats that lightly. In fact it causes quite a stir and a lot of bad publicity.

Other Information

Published accounts contain other information, much of which is in the form of notes explaining, or giving more details of, items in the balance sheet and profit and loss accounts. The following are of special interest:

- List of directors' fees and other payments.
- List of the number of employees earning salaries over £30 000 in bands of £5000.
- The average number of employees and total remuneration.
- Details of loans.
- Details of fixed assets.
- List of subsidiary companies and related companies.
- Main countries of operation.
- Geographical analysis of turnover and trading results.
- A statement of the accounting policies that have been used.

This is not meant to be an exhaustive list of what you will find in company accounts. As we noted on p. 57, if the information is not there then the company was not obliged to publish it!

Review

The quiz below is designed to refresh your memory about the accounting procedures covered in Part I. Each question has three possible answers of which only one is correct. Tick whichever answer you think sounds most likely to be correct and then check your answers with the true ones on p. 85.

Company Accounts Quiz

1 A balance sheet is:
- **a** something to keep you from falling out of bed;
- **b** a statement of the capital and assets of a firm;
- **c** something that shows how a firm's profit or loss was made.

2 Assets are:
- **a** things of value in a firm;
- **b** money owed by a firm;
- **c** the money put in by shareholders.

3 Fixed assets are:
a articles riveted to the ground;
b money borrowed over a long period;
c items of value in a firm of lasting value.
4 A car is:
a a fixed asset;
b a current asset;
c a liability.
5 Current assets are:
a stocks + debtors + cash;
b the value of light bulbs;
c the amount of money a firm owes the bank.
6 Debtors are:
a people in prison;
b the amount of money owed by a firm;
c the amount of money owed to a firm.
7 Equity is another name in business for:
a the bosses' trade union;
b the owners' capital;
c the balance sheet.
8 Equity is made up of:
a assets +liabilities;
b share capital + retained profits + other reserves;
c share capital + current liabilities.
9 Debt is another word for:
a share capital;
b borrowed capital;
c current assets.
10 A current liability is:
a borrowed capital to be paid back soon;
b the share capital;
c debtors + cash.
11 Creditors are:
a a form of long-term borrowing;
b the same as debtors;
c a current liability.
12 A bank overdraft is:
a a current liability;
b the difference between current assets and current liabilities;
c a bank's air-conditioning system
13 Net profit after tax is used for:
a interest, dividends and tax;
b tax and retained profit;
c dividends and retained profit.

14 Interest is deducted from profit:
- **a** before tax;
- **b** after tax;
- **c** never.

15 Depreciation is:
- **a** the cost of a fire;
- **b** the permanent loss of value of a fixed asset;
- **c** a slanderous remark.

16 Reducing-balance depreciation:
- **a** has a small amount of depreciation gradually increasing over the years;
- **b** is the same amount each year;
- **c** is high in the early years and gradually diminishes.

17 Which of these statements about the balance sheet is most accurate:
- **a** A balance sheet is a detailed statement accurately stating the real value of the firm.
- **b** The balance sheet shows the values of assets and capital employed over a year.
- **c** The balance sheet shows the assets of a firm and its capital at a moment in time.

18 Gearing is:
- **a** something to do with fashion;
- **b** the relationship between equity capital and borrowed capital;
- **c** the difference between assets and current liabilities.

19 If a company changes the value of its assets to take account of inflation its profitability will usually be:
- **a** unaffected;
- **b** higher;
- **c** lower.

20 In the source and application of funds statement, depreciation is considered to be:
- **a** an outflow of funds;
- **b** an inflow of funds;
- **c** a neat way of balancing the account.

21 If trade creditors are increased between the beginning and end of the year, then this is the same as:
- **a** a reckless gamble;
- **b** a source of funds;
- **c** a use of funds.

22 Which of the following is not true (only one)?
- **a** An increase in stock levels is an outflow of funds.
- **b** An increase in debtors is an inflow.
- **c** Expenditure on fixed assets is an outflow.

23 In current cost accounting, the depreciation adjustment is:
a a way of reducing the value of assets;
b a more realistic sum to set aside for growth;
c a more realistic sum to set aside for replacement of assets.

24 The cost of sales adjustment is something to do with:
a fixing prices;
b making more profit;
c revaluing stocks to allow for inflation.

25 Monetary working capital is:
a debtors less creditors;
b a bribe to get someone to work on a building;
c current assets less current liabilities.

26 Value added is a value representing:
a the wealth created by a company;
b the money available for growth;
c something to do with tax.

27 Value added is a sum:
a greater than turnover;
b less than turnover;
c about the same as turnover.

28 In a company the stakeholders are:
a butchers;
b vampire hunters;
c anyone with an interest in the company in the financial sense.

29 A limited company is:
a not permitted to grow;
b short for 'having limited liability';
c unprofitable.

30 A company's auditors are:
a independent and act for the shareholders;
b an expensive luxury;
c an internal telephone system.

Answers

Scoring You get one mark for every correct answer with a maximum of 30 marks.

1 b; 2 a; 3 c; 4 a; 5 a; 6 c; 7 b; 8 b; 9 b; 10 a; 11 c; 12 a; 13 c; 14 a; 15 b; 16 c; 17 c; 18 b; 19 c; 20 b; 21 b; 22 b; 23 c; 24 c; 25 a; 26 a; 27 b; 28 c; 29 b; 30 a.

If you had between 23 and 30 correct answers, you have nothing to fear from accounts. If you completed the quiz in under ten minutes as well, you are on the way to being a good auditor. Slower, a good accountant.

A score of 16 to 22 puts you in the very good league of accounts readers who are likely to ask awkward questions at company meetings.

If you scored 9 to 15 you have enough knowledge to surprise your friends and be able to communicate with most accountants (at last).

A score of 8 or less means you are probably a very rich businessman who does not care – if not, check out where you went wrong (both in business and in the quiz).

Part II

Accounts – Evaluation and Interpretation

We should now be able to describe the contents of a company's accounts and be able to say what the words mean. However, it is possible to get considerably more out of a company's accounts if you know what to look for and how to analyse them. This part of the book deals with the techniques of analysis and also identifies the limitations of accounts. We shall be looking at a company's accounts in detail, as well as looking at how things are done in the USA.

9 Accounts Analysis (1) – Growth and Profitability

The aim of this chapter and the next is to show you what questions you can reasonably ask about a company's accounts, and how you can go about finding the answers, so that you will be able to pick up any set of accounts and comment on them. We will first focus on growth and profitability.

Have you ever thought what you would do if you suddenly came into a lot of money? It does happen quite often these days, for instance either by winning a competition or (occasionally) by gambling, or as a result of an early retirement scheme at work. The first decision is usually how much of it to spend? After that the question to ask is: 'Where should I invest the money.' Let us suppose that you decide to invest £30 000 in a small business, so that you will have a job as well as a source of income and you decide to buy a bookshop.

What would you want to know about the business before you made an offer for it, assuming that the shop is in a good position and has no immediate competition?

You would certainly want to know if the business was making a profit and how big a profit it was making. Moreover you would need to know if you would be able to earn a reasonable living from it – there would not be much point in working very hard and ending up poorer than when you started. Another important element in the equation is how much growth there has been over the last few years; you don't buy a firm that is shrinking. This might lead to the question of the prospects for the future – is it likely to grow? Of course nobody can predict what will happen in the future but a reasonable estimate has to be made. One other fundamental question to ask is how much does the present owner want for the business and whether the goodwill amounts to much. A valuation of the assets would be included in the price. What exactly are the assets and are there a lot of them or only a little? Here is a list of some of the other questions you might ask:

- What kinds of book sell best? Which are most profitable?
- How many staff are employed and how much are they paid?

- How much does the present owner take out of the business?
- What is the rest of the money spent on? Is this excessive or reasonable?
- Are there are debtors and is the figure reasonable?
- Does the business owe any money? If so, to whom and are the amounts reasonable?

You have decided to buy the business and, after haggling, you are asked to pay £50 000 for it. You go to the bank manager for a loan to cover the difference. What do you think the bank will want to know about the firm on top of all the information you have already asked about?

Here are some certain questions:

- How much interest could the firm pay?
- If the business went broke how would the bank get its money back?
- How much would be a safe amount to lend? What are the chances of the bank losing its money?
- Is the present level of borrowing too high?

All these questions are bound to be asked by the bank manager – indeed anyone lending money would be foolish not to ask them.

It will now be obvious that a lot of questions should be asked before a business is bought or before money is lent to a business. Indeed the same questions can be asked even if the intention is merely to invest in a company, or simply to sell it. To sum up all of these in a sentence, it can be said that the aim of any such exercise is:

to take an investment decision, having considered the likely level of risk *and the likely level of* reward.

Risk can be defined as the possibility of ending up worse off than when you started. Reward is the expected return (or profit) you are likely to get back.

Activity

Suppose you had £1000 to spare and you wanted to try to increase it by investing it in one of these four options:

- Backing a horse at 100 to 1.
- Putting it on deposit in the bank at 9% interest.
- Buying 400 shares in British Petroleum at £2.50 each.
- Buying a stake in a company set up to look for gold in Central America.

Which of the four investments would yield the best return if everything worked out well very quickly and which is the most risky? Rank all four investments according to these two criteria with 1 denoting lowest and 4 for highest:

	Risk	*Return*
Horse race		
Bank deposit		
BP shares		
Gold prospecting		

You have probably discovered that the rankings reveal a pattern – the highest return goes with the highest risk and the lowest return ties in with the lowest risk. A horse race, betting on odds of 100 to 1, is the most risky yet it could yield the best return. The bank deposit is the safest (at least in a reputable bank), but the return is lowest. BP shares are more risky than the bank deposit, because the value of the shares could fall and the dividend paid out could be less than 9%. However, both the price of the share and the dividend could rise to give a very good total return. Finally the gold prospecting company is very risky, but not so chancy as the horse. Neither is it likely to yield such a good return – but it could be a lot more rewarding than the BP shares.

The decision on which alternative to go for is a matter for individual taste, but the starting point must always be the same, namely, *get the facts* – and with a company the facts are first revealed in the accounts. It must be stressed, however, that the accounts do not tell the whole story. Other sources of information have to be used as well, but the accounts are the best starting point.

There are two kinds of facts in company accounts: the obvious and those that have to be uncovered. An obvious fact is one which answers the question directly. For example, in the list of questions that were posed on p. 90 some like 'Were there any debtors?' and 'Did the business owe any money?' had obvious answers. These are easily obtained facts; but some of the questions were much trickier such as: 'Was the debtors' figure reasonable?' and 'Were the amounts owed by the firm reasonable?' If we want the facts to answer those questions we have to do a bit of digging – it's rather like a treasure hunt: some facts, some clues and then the search and a dig.

9.1 Analysis – the Four Key Steps

Classify the Questions

The list of question we developed on p. 90 covered many different aspects of the business. There were questions on costs, questions on assets, while others were related to profits and so on. It is easier if the questions are grouped into categories to start with so that you can focus your attention on one aspect of the company at a time. The categories are:

- Growth.
- Profitability (or returns).
- Financial strength (the bank's questions on p. 90).
- Assets.
- Borrowings (or financial structure).
- Operational efficiency.

All the questions on p. 90 can be fitted into these six categories, except that relating to the company's prospects.

Treat the Numbers

Drawing conclusions from untreated figures is a dangerous and difficult activity. For example, try to draw conclusions from these bits of information:

- Last Saturday Manchester United attracted 26 573 spectators to their match with Everton.
- A supermarket in Edinburgh had a turnover last week of £245 000.
- One of the North Sea oilfields produces 109 700 barrels of oil a day.

If you had trouble coming to any conclusions about these numbers it is not surprising, since you were not given enough information to be able to form a sensible opinion. Moreover, the numbers themselves were fairly big and hard to handle. The way out is, first, to reduce the numbers to a manageable size and then to convert them to *ratios*.

Reducing the numbers to a manageable size is easy – just round the numbers to three or four significant figures, so that the number of spectators becomes 26 $\frac{1}{2}$ thousand, the oil production figure is 110 thousand barrels and the turnover of the supermarket is £ $\frac{1}{4}$ million. Much easier to grasp, aren't they?

Next, the numbers need to be turned to ratios. A ratio is a way of showing the size of a number relative to another number and the commonest type is percentage. For example, the statements above would be much more helpful if it was stated that the attendance at the football match was 47.5% of capacity, that the oilfield produced 53% of total North Sea output and that the supermarket's turnover was up 9% on the previous week.

A ratio, therefore, describes a *significant relationship* and is essential for the next step of the hunt.

Compare

The three statements made in the last paragraph still do not mean very much because it is impossible to draw any interesting conclusions from them. However, if there were some other statistics with which we could compare these figures, we really would be able to say something interesting.

Here are some comparative statistics relating to the three examples we have been discussing. Spend a few minutes looking at each item and try to come to a conclusion about them.

- The average attendance figure at Manchester United of 39 000 is 70% of capacity.
- Several oilfields each produce over 10% of total North Seas output, but the average is less than 80 000 barrels a day.
- On average the turnover of all supermarkets rose last year by 5% although the best 25% increased by more than 15%.

Draw your Conclusions

The conclusions you have arrived at now are most likely to be a lot better than any views you may have had at the start. By now the conclusion about the football match is that it was not very well attended. The oilfield is fairly large but by no means the biggest. As for the supermarket, it is better than average but far from having the best growth rate.

Now that we have had a look at the way to analyse accounts, the next job is to identify the key ratios that will actually help us to hunt the truth. The six categories of questions we identified on p. 92 will be looked at in turn, looking at growth and profitability in this chapter and the others in Chapter 10.

9.2 Growth

It is often best to start with the question: 'Has the company grown?' If the answer is 'No' or 'Not a lot' then the conclusion is that there must be some kind of problem, unless you know that the company actually has a policy of no growth. Even then you will no want to put money into it if you are looking for growth yourself.

How is growth measured? The simplest way would be to compare the volume sold in the first year with the volume sold in the second year, like this:

Volume sold in 1989	2 600 tons
Volume sold in 1988	2 000 tons
Increase	600 tons

Therefore the increase in tons sold is $(600 \div 2000) \times 100 = 30\%$.

As we saw in the last chapter (p. 77), volume is often very difficult to obtain in any sensible form; only if the item being compared is exactly the same from one year to another is the comparison valid.

What is wrong with the following comparison? Can you see the trap for the unwary? 'My local garage sells a wide range of motorcars. Last year it sold 15% more cars than it did the year before.'

The comparison is valid only if the range of cars sold in both years was exactly the same and, moreover, they sold cars in exactly the same proportions as before. As it stands they could have sold fewer big cars and many more small cars, ending up with no monetary growth at all.

The obvious alternative to volume is to use turnover. This is always available but, as we saw when we looked at value added, it is sometimes unduly affected by the cost of bought materials (remember Roger's Coffee Imports on p. 76?). In such cases it is helpful to use the value added figure, especially if the comparison you are going to make is against some general growth statistics – such as the rate of growth of the economy as a whole.

Other useful growth figures to calculate are:

- Total assets.
- Equity capital (measuring the rate of growth of the company itself).
- Earnings.
- Physical items such as staff, operating units (e.g., lorries, branches, shops).

With growth figures it is helpful also to calculate the statistics for a four- or five-year period because it is risky to look at just one year's growth rate.

What do you make of these growth statistics?

	Sales (tons)	*Increase* (%)
1985	1 000	–
1986	1 050	5.0
1987	1 113	6.0
1988	1 124	1.0
1989	1 251	11.3

Obviously something odd happened in 1988, and the effect was to make the 1989 growth rate look a lot better than that of the previous year. If we had been looking at the increase from 1988 to 1989 only, we might have easily drawn a wrong conclusion about the general rate of growth.

9.3 Profitability

It is not difficult for a company to make a profit. To make an adequate profit is harder, and to generate a more than satisfactory profit is fairly difficult (and fairly rare). It is easy to see whether a company has or has not made a profit, but it is not possible to tell by a quick glance at the accounts whether the profit is either adequate or satisfactory. Measures of profitability are designed to help us decide.

Several measures are in common use, so if you are told that a firm's profitability is x%, always ask for a definition. The most commonly used numerators (i.e. the numbers on top of fractions) for the profitability ratio are:

- Operating profit.
- Earnings (profit after tax, before or after deducting extraordinary items).
- Dividends.

The most used denominators (i.e. numbers on the bottom line of fractions) are:

- Assets employed (this can be total assets, or only operating assets, i.e. those used for trading purposes).
- Capital employed (total capital is the same as total assets).
- Equity capital.
- Number of issued shares.

Frequently the expression used to describe these ratios starts with the words 'return on . . .' and so you will see:

- Return on assets (ROA). This is usually (operating profit ÷ total assets) %.
- Return on capital employed (ROC or ROCE). If total capital is being used, the profit to refer to will be before tax and interest payments. If equity capital is used, it is better to relate profit after tax to that. This is also called:
- Return on equity (ROE).
- Return of net assets (RONA).

You may also find the expressions 'return on investment' (ROI) used. This is most often used in business planning to describe the profits that are expected from an investment and is calculated to see if the investment will be worthwhile.

All these ratios are trying to measure the same thing, namely, how effectively the company has used the financial resources available to it during the year. This can be compared to you or me deciding where to invest £50 that we have spare: we would look at the different interest rates that are on offer from the banks, building societies, Post Office or National Savings; other things being equal, we would invest where we would obtain the best return on our money. With a company, and after the year has ended, we want to know whether its management successfully used the money entrusted to it – or whether it would have made more sense to give up and put the money in the bank instead. Here are the relevant figures for three companies to illustrate the point:

Company	*A*	*B*	*C*
	£000	£000	£000
Operating profit	50	80	100
Less interest	10	—	40
	40	80	60
Less tax	20	40	30
Earnings	20	40	30
Total assets	500	400	400
Equity capital	400	300	100

For each of the companies above, calculate the following profitability ratios and then decide which is the most profitable and which is the least profitable.

	A	*B*	*C*
	%	%	%
1 (Operating profit ÷ total assets) × 100			
2 (Net profit after tax ÷ equity capital)– × 100			

Company *C* comes out on top, with an operating return of 25% and a return on equity of 30%. Poor old company *A* can only manage a return on equity of 5% with a return on total assets of 10%. Company *B* has a return on assets of 20% and a return on equity of 13.3%.

Capital and Asset Values – Which to Use?

There is a problem in calculating profitability ratios because several different numbers could be used for the assets or capital part of the formula. It is traditional to compile the ratio by relating profit for the year to the value of capital in the balance sheet at the *end* of that year. However, in reality, profits are made by the assets or capital in use over the year as a whole and therefore some kind of average should be used to get a better measure of profitability. For example, a firm that raised a large loan just before the year-end would show an increase in its assets.

However, these assets would not have had time to make any money and so the return on assets figure would be lower than if the loan had been negotiated after the year-end.

Some writers consider that the asset values at the beginning of the year should be used for the denominator of the ratios, but there is not much support for this method. If you want to use an average instead, add the values at the start and the end of the year and then simply divide by two.

A further problem arises in relation to the valuation of assets to take account of inflation. If we use the historic cost valuation (as most people do) we are comparing this year's profits with assets valued at 'yesterday's' prices. It is much more precise to use asset values that are up to date. Using the historic cost basis tends to make profitability ratios higher than they really are, so be very careful in making a comparison between a return on assets ratio for a company and the rate of interest available from the bank or from government stocks.

Other Profitability Measures

The ratios involving dividends and the amount of profit earned in relation to the shares themselves are of particular interest to shareholders. These ratios are earnings per share (EPS) and dividend ratios:

Earnings Per Share

There is an official definition for this (see SSAP3):

> profit after tax, after deducting minority interests and preference dividends, but before taking into account extraordinary items
>
> *divided by*
>
> number of equity shares at the date of the balance sheet entitled to dividends.

The answer is normally shown in Britain as a certain number of pence per share (see p. 125 for an example).

This ratio is much more popular in the USA than in Britain, where a company's progress each quarter is marked by the change in the EPS. It is, however, difficult to get a good idea of a company's real progress in times of inflation because the earnings figure will be bigger, not because of efficiency but because of rising prices. Another limitation of EPS is that it cannot be used for comparing one company against another. This is partly due to the fact that the nominal value of a share can vary from 5p to £1. Clearly, an EPS of 25p on shares of 5p is a very different proposition to an EPS of 25p on shares of £1. Comparison is also made difficult because of the way taxation affects earnings. This is very technical and need not concern you here.

Dividend Ratios

Three ratios involving dividends are important:

Dividend per share

This is calculated by dividing the total dividends payable to shareholders in a year by the actual number of shares entitled to receive it. It is a quick way of seeing how a firm has been doing and is useful for investors since they can quickly work out how much dividend they will receive – assuming they know how many shares they have (see p. 125).

Dividend %

This is simply the dividend per share divided by the nominal value of the share. So that if a company with 50p shares gives dividends of 10p during the year, it has given a dividend of 20%. This is not used so much these days, but is helpful if looked at over a few years as it indicates how well the shareholders have been rewarded over time.

Dividend cover

This ratio is calculated in this way:

earnings per share ÷ dividend per share.

It is called dividend 'cover' because it shows how much of the profit is being taken out of the firm and whether the cost of the dividend is well secured.

Note that if the dividend cover is less than 1.00, the firm is paying some of the dividend out of reserves. For example, if a company has a dividend cover of 0.8, and the figures on which the ratio was calculated were: earnings £80 000, dividend £100 000, you may see a problem. Similarly, a very low ratio (e.g., 1.0 to 2.5) suggests either low earnings or a high pay-out level. Either way the firm may not be ploughing enough money back into the business.

Stock Market Profitability Indicators

Where a company has its shares quoted on the stock market, another set of ratios can be calculated which use the current market price of the shares. Although this figure is not usually quoted in the accounts, the ratios that can be calculated with it are important. Here is a brief description of the main ones (a source of detailed information on these ratios will be found in the reading list at the end of the book).

Dividend yield

The formula for this ratio is:

(dividend per share × 100) ÷ market price per share.

If I buy a share at £3.60 and I receive a dividend of 18p then the yield is 5%, clearly an important thing to look at in taking an investment decision.

Price-earnings ratio (or p/e ratio)
This formula is:

market price per share ÷ earnings per share.

If a company has its shares valued at £3.60 and its EPS is 30p then its p/e ratio is twelve times. The popularity of this ratio has declined in recent years with changes in the way tax is calculated. Moreover, there is no general agreement as to its utility. However, a very high p/e is a sign of a popular share – one with 'prospects'.

Earnings yield
This ratio is the p/e ratio turned upside down. It used to be popular and is calculated like this:

(earnings per share × 100) ÷ market price per share.

In the example we used for the p/e ratio, the earnings yield works out at 8.3%. Some potential investors look for companies with a high earnings yield, since it may be a sign of a low-priced share. Profits are high in relation to the market's valuation of the firm, so there is a chance of a good dividend yield or a rise in the share price.

Return on shareholder's capital (ROSC)
Shareholders obtain their return in two ways, from dividends and from the growth in the value of the share itself. ROSC is therefore:

((dividends + change in share price) ÷ purchase price of share) × 100.

If I buy a share at £3.60 and receive a dividend of 18p, then sell the share for £4.14, what is the ROSC %?

The price of the share rose from £3.60 to £4.14 while I owned it, so its value increased by 54p, and by adding the dividend of 18p I obtained a total return of 72p, which is 20% of the original investment.

Warning
In all the ratios that use current market prices, always remember that today's price is being compared to yesterday's profits – and there is no guarantee that they will be as good next year.

What is an Adequate Return?
An adequate rate of return on capital (however measured) is vital for any business that wants to thrive. It is necessary for the following reasons:

- To reward the shareholders who have risked and tied up their money.
- To provide funds for the development and growth of the business.
- To provide security for the employees and the lenders, as well as the firm's suppliers.
- To make it possible to attract new funds from outside.
- To be able to pay for next year's goods and services at inflated prices, without reducing reserves.

There is no single percentage which serves as a yardstick for 'adequate'. However, there are some very general sources of information that may help:

- Look at the rate of interest that banks are offering. This is really a minimum rate of return and, the more risky the business, the higher should be the return.
- The *Financial Times* publishes many statistics relating to companies with shares on the stock market.
- The magazine *Management Today* publishes, each 5 June, a 'profitability league table' showing the latest return on equity figures for the 200 largest British companies. An interesting table, but it only includes companies with shares on the British stock market and uses historic costs as the basis.
- The American magazine *Fortune* publishes a very detailed set of profitability league tables, called 'The Fortune 500', each May and also a second 500 listing and a world league table.
- The *Financial Times* also publishes a European 500 survey which contains ROCE ratios and other statistics.
- All the above are using information from published accounts and subject to all the conditions we have discussed. If you want to be any more precise, you have to look at the accounts yourself and calculate the ratios using your own definitions which you must stick to all the time.
- If you have a business of your own, you may be able to obtain detailed ratios about other firms in your industry or trade by taking part in an 'interfirm comparison' scheme organized by your trade association or by the Centre for Interfirm Comparison. These schemes are the only ones where the ratios are really comparable from one firm to another.

A Final Note on Profitability and Growth

When you look at lists of profitability and growth, you will always find a wide range of results. Some firms will have no growth and negative rates of return, with zero dividends and a poor market rating. Others will be at the other end of the league table, with high rates of return, a fast rate of growth, an excellent dividend record and doing well on the stock market.

Most firms will not be so obviously good or bad, but even so, the best yardstick to follow is that of the best ten or twenty firms in the league. By definition, all the rest are unsuccessful.

10 Accounts Analysis (2) – Assets, Operations and Financial

The analysis of profitability and growth we considered in the last chapter helps us to gain an appreciation of where the company stands in terms of its overall performance, since the measures we discussed are all common indicators of commercial success. It is, however, important to probe beneath the surface to see if there is any sign of weakness which may affect the future success of the firm and also to be able to identify the factors which have influenced the company in the past.

The main areas to investigate are the firm's financial strength, its assets, its financial structure and its operational efficiency.

10.1 Financial Strength

The third group of questions we identified on p. 92 which can be asked about a company relate to what I have called 'financial strength' and what are sometimes described as 'financial health' measures. The answers to questions like this help us to decide whether the company is in any danger of being short of money and of not being able to pay bills or meet debts. Several ratios are commonly calculated to do this job for us; some are called 'liquidity ratios' and others are known as 'financial cover ratios'. For instance, if you had £5 in your pocket, £50 in the bank and nothing else you could turn into money quickly, and you owed £100 to the Electricity Board which had to be paid by the end of the week, what words would you use to describe your financial situation? Would it make any difference if you were going to receive £500 in wages at the end of the week?

You might well describe your position as desperate if no income was due, but where money was expected the situation could be described as embarrassing. In accountants' languauge, 'there is a liquidity problem'.

Accountants use two ratios to look at liquidity: the current ratio and the acid-test (or quick) ratio.

The Current Ratio (Working Capital Ratio)

This ratio takes current liabilities as its starting point.

If you look back at the current liabilities figure for Sam's business on p. 43, you will see that all the money that Sam owed had to be paid off soon, probably within the next month or two. What would he use to pay off those liabilities?

In a word, he will pay off his debts with cash. Once the cash is used up, though, other sources of money have to be tapped, which means converting other assets into a 'liquid form'. Once cash has been used and any money invested has been withdrawn, the next easiest source is the firm's debtors. After that, stocks of finished goods get converted to sales and then cash, and if there is any work in progress or stocks of materials, these would get turned into saleable goods, sold and eventually they too would produce cash.

The current ratio relates a firm's current liabilities to its current assets to indicate its ability at a point in time to pay off its immediate debts. It is calculated as:

current assets ÷ current liabilities.

For example, using Sam's working capital statement on p. 43, we get:

current assets ÷ current liabilities = £3100 ÷ £2800 = 1.11 (approximately).

This ratio means that the current liabilities are covered by the current assets 1.11 times – or (on the face of it) at that point in time there were adequate current assets to pay for current liabilities.

What is a 'good' size for the current ratio? The answer is: it all depends on the company and how successful it is, what its record is like – looking at the same ratio over several years – and what is considered to be 'normal' for the industry.

Shops tend to have very low figures because they do not tie up much money in current assets; there are neither debtors nor work in progress. Heavy engineering firms will usually have stocks of materials and finished goods as well as debtors and work in progress, and their current ratio will be very high by comparison. The current ratio for GEC was 1.73 at 31 march 1985, whereas the comparable Tesco figure was 0.61.

The Acid-test Ratio

There is a snag with the current ratio as a measure of liquidity, namely, that stocks and work in progress may not easily be converted to money. In other words they are relatively 'illiquid'. For example, GEC had about 20% of its current assets tied up in either work in progress or in contracts in progress, i.e. incompleted construction work. None of these could be turned to cash quickly. If a firm is in a hurry to raise money it may have to sell its stocks of materials and finished goods at less than their book value, so these elements in current assets are not usually considered to be liquid assets. In fact liquid assets are cash + debtors + short-term investments, and it is these that are available for paying off current liabilities. The ratio is therefore:

liquid assets ÷ current liabilities.

In Sam's shop the ratio works out at £2300 ÷ £2800 = 0.82 times. Sometimes this ratio is called 'the quick ratio' because it shows the ability of the firm to pay off its current liabilities quickly. Banks in particular look hard at this ratio whenever a business asks for a loan or overdraft.

Look at the figures below for a minute or two, calculate the two ratios we have been discussing and then decide if you would lend the firm the money it needs to pay the taxman. You have been told that at least £800 will come into the business during the next few weeks.

Current assets	
Stocks	3 420
Debtors	900
Cash	–
Total	4 320
Current liabilities	
Trade creditors	2 300
Tax due	700
Overdraft	600
Total	£3 600

The current ratio is 1.20 times, which is not unacceptable as it stands. The acid-test ratio is, however, very low at 0.25 times. If you lent the £700 needed to pay the taxman and then £800 did come in, the business is still in a very illiquid situation and practically insolvent (insolvent means unable to pay debts when due).

Interest Cover Ratio

The interest cover ratio looks at another aspect of the borrowing problem – namely, the ability of the firm to pay interest on the money it has borrowed. The ratio is calculated thus:

total profit ÷ interest paid.

(Total profit = trading profit + other income.)

Consider the relevant information for two similar-sized companies:

	Firm P	*Firm Q*
	£000	£000
Operating profit + other income	650	750
Less: interest paid	130	300
Net profit before tax	520	450
Interest cover	5.00	2.50

The problem for Firm Q is that if its operation profits fell and it still had the same amount of interest to pay, it could end up in a very embarrassing position; after paying the interest and tax, it might not have much left for the shareholders or to retain in the firm. A fall of 40% in total profit for Firm P would leave it with pre-tax profits of £260 000 – a 50% drop. On the other hand, a 40% fall in total profit for Firm Q would leave it with pre-tax profits of only £150 000 – a 67% drop.

You may see this ratio upside down and shown as a percentage, in which case it is called the 'income gearing ratio'.

Loan Cover

Another aspect of the financial strength of a company is its ability to pay back borrowings. In particular, if a company wants to borrow for a medium- or long-term period, the lender usually seeks some kind of security for the loan. This applies to individuals as well as firms and, if you want to borrow to buy a house, for example, you will not be able to get a loan for more than the current value of the property. Indeed, between 80% and 90% of the value is the norm for house purchase loans.

With a company the ratio is:

Fixed assets (as written-down book value) ÷
All medium- and long-term debt
(creditors falling due after one year)

Here is an example of two companies with widely differing loan cover ratios. It is not difficult to see which could borrow more, assuming that profits and prospects are similar:

	Firm Y	*Firm Z*
	£000	£000
Fixed assets	250	550
Loans (more than one year)	25	110
Loan cover	10.0	5.0

Firm Y has a high ratio compared with Firm Z, but neither is very low – the situation begins to look difficult when loans are 50% of fixed assets.

A variant of this ratio compares all assets (excluding the intangibles) and relates it to all debt:

tangible assets ÷ total debt

10.2 Assets

The next category of ratios to calculate helps us to understand a little more about where the company has tied up its money, and how well or badly it is using its assets.

A Case to Consider
There were two shops selling bicycles and at the end of the year both had tangible assets of £60 000 including the shop itself. The first shop had made sales of £80 000 during the year, with a profit after tax of £8000. The second shop had only managed a turnover of £60 000 and its profit after tax was £6000. Both shops were of similar size and of similar age and condition. It is not difficult to work out which of the two shops was using its assets best. Since both shops were of similar size and had similar asset values, the relatively low turnover of the second shop points to poor asset utilization. The ratio that measures this is:?

sales ÷ assets.

and the figure for shop 1 is: £80 000 ÷ £60 000 = 1.33 times, whereas shop 2 has £60 000 ÷ £60 000 = 1.00 times. In other words, shop 1 is turning its assets over faster than shop 2; it is utilizing its assets better.

An alternative ratio to express this idea is:

(assets ÷ sales) × 1000.

The figures for the two shops are: shop 1, £750; shop 2, £1000. This shows that shop 1 needs £750 of assets to generate £1000 of sales, whereas shop 2 needs £1000 of assets to generate £1000 of sales. The neat thing about this particular ratio is that it can be used for all asset items:

(Stocks ÷ sales) × 1000 +
(Debtors ÷ sales) × 1000
= **(Current assets ÷ sales)** × 1000

and

(Land and buildings ÷ sales) × 1000 +
(Plant and machinery ÷ sales) ÷ 1000
= **(Fixed assets ÷ sales)** × 1000

Also:

(Current assets ÷ sales) × 1000 +
(Fixed assets ÷ sales) × 1000
= **(Total assets ÷ sales)** × 1000.

Each of these asset utilisation ratios shows the amount of money tied up in the particular asset for every £1000 of sales generated.

Below, you will see the assets of a company over a two-year period together with the sales figures. Following this, the asset utilisation ratios have been calculated and by comparing one year's ratios with another, you will very quickly be able to see where the company is not utilising its assets as well as before.

	Year 1	*Year 2*
	£000	£000
Material stocks	100	120
Work in progress	20	30
Finished goods stocks	40	50
Debtors	120	180
Current assets	280	380
Land and buildings	60	70
Plant and machinery	160	200
Fixed assets	220	270
Total assets	£500	£650
Sales	£1000	£1200

	Year 1	*Year 2*
	£ per £1 000	£ per £1 000
Material stocks	100	100
Work in progress	20	25
Finished goods stocks	40	42
Debtors	120	150
Current assets	280	317
Land and buildings	60	58
Plant and machinery	160	167
Fixed assets	220	225
Total assets	500	542

The ratios highlight the fact that several items are moving the wrong way – work in progress has risen significantly and there has been a small rise in the finished goods and plant and machinery ratios. However, the main cause of the poor situation is the very big increase in debtors, not in absolute terms but in relation to sales.

Other Asset Ratios

In addition to the ratios we have been looking at, there are some others which can make our analysis even better, although it may not be possible to get the information needed in some circumstances:

Debtors

(Debtors ÷ sales) × 365.

This shows the average number of days customers take to pay up. In the example we have just worked the days are 44 in year 1 and 55 in year 2 (approximately).

Materials stocks

(Materials stocks ÷ cost of materials used) × 365.

This shows the average number of days usage of materials in hand.

Finished goods stocks

(Finished goods stocks ÷ production cost of goods made) × 365.

This tells you how many days sales equivalent there is in stock.

Asset Turnover – Fast or Slow?

If a company has a very fast turnover of assets, it either has very few assets or its sales are very high. For example, a firm that rents all its fixed assets will have a faster asset turnover than one with all its equipment and buildings owned. If a firm has modern machinery it will not have such a fast asset turnover as the company with fully depreciated assets.

For example, a supermarket's assets are small – it has few debtors and low stocks, as well as little equipment. Its asset turnover will therefore be high, as will the asset turnover in a labour-intensive company which has little by way of machinery and equipment. An advertising agency would have a fast asset turnover too.

In contrast to this type of company, firms with a slow asset turnover include expensive jewellery shops, motor-car manufacturers and all capital-intensive firms.

Finally, a very successful company which is working round the clock and operating at full capacity is going to have a much faster asset turnover than the firm which is having a hard time selling its products and has spare capacity.

10.3 **Financial Structure**

The ratios we have been looking at are fairly straightforward because they are describing and analysing asset structure. The other side of the balance sheet – that relating to capital – is more complex, and in many ways more significant when it comes to evaluating risk. The important fact to establish is how much of the company's assets have been bought with equity capital and how much with borrowed money. There is a simple ratio to measure this:

debt ÷ equity = the 'gearing' ratio

Here are three sets of figures for three firms in the same line of business:

	Company A	*Company B*	*Company C*
	£000	£000	£000
Equity capital	600	400	300
Borrowed capital	400	600	700
Total capital (total assets)	1 000	1 000	1 000
(Debt ÷ equity)%	0.67	1.50	2.33

The profit and loss accounts for the three firms will look like this:

	A	*B*	*C*
Trading profit	250	£250	£250
Less interest (at 9%)	36	54	63
Profit before tax	£214	£196	£187
(Profit ÷ equity)%	35.7	49.0	62.3

It is clear, therefore, that the firm with the highest gearing has the best return on equity and the firm that has borrowed least has the lowest return. You will, of course, remember the problem with a high level of borrowing that we discussed on p. 105 (the interest cover ratio); namely, if profits fall substantially, the firm with the highest level of borrowing is most at risk. So the message about gearing is:

- *high gearing is good for the shareholders in times of a high level of activity, but is bad when things are not going so well.*

There are other ways of calculating gearing. Those which use the balance sheet figures are called 'capital gearing ratios', and those which use the profit and interest payments figures from the profit and loss account are called 'income gearing ratios'. Both types are used to obtain a good picture of a company's gearing and its 'exposure to financial risk'.

It is very difficult to generalise about what is an acceptable level of gearing. It depends on the company, its products, the markets it's in, the state of the industry and the economy, and how much risk the owners and the directors of the firm are prepared to take. If they do not borrow and have a very low level of gearing, they are said to be 'risk-averse'.

10.4 **Operating Efficiency**

In the examples above, we assumed that the three firms were equally efficient. Naturally this does not happen all that often in reality and it is important to find out why one company is better than another, or indeed why operating efficiency might have deteriorated from one year to another, unless the company is complacent – a recipe for disaster!

The starting point is usually the profitability ratio, which looks at the results of the firm at the trading level. What are then needed are some ratios that will explain how that level of profitability has been achieved and why it is different (either from the previous year or as against other firms).

The Two Props of Profitability

The level of profitability in any company is determined by two key factors. These are the overall utilisation of assets that we have already seen and a very well-known concept – the 'profit margin on sales'.

The ratio that measures profit margins is:

(trading profit ÷ sales) × 100

and when calculated it shows just how much profit has been made from £100 of sales.

Below you will see the sales, operating profits and profit margins for two firms in the same business:

	Posh Café Ltd	*Fred's Fast Foods*
	£000	£000
Sales	400	800
Operating (trading) profit	60	60

The profit margin on the Posh Café operations is 15%, whereas for Fred's Fast Foods it is only 7.5%. Both are making the same amount of profit but the first firm is achieving its results on half the turnover. There are a variety of reasons why one company should have a higher profit margin than another and it is possible to get some clues by looking at the ratios relating to costs. You will remember that sales – costs = profit. Or costs + profit = sales. In the same way, (profit ÷ sales)% + (costs ÷ sales)% = 100%. So a firm with a profit margin of 15% of sales must have total costs of 85% of sales.

Many cost ratios can be calculated, and listed below are some of the common cost items used to calculate these ratios – usually with sales (sometimes value added) as the denominator:

- Cost of goods sold (and gross profit).
- Total wages.
- Distribution costs.
- Selling costs.
- Production costs.
- Overheads.

The main difficulty with cost ratios is that the information needed is not always given in the published accounts. Internally the figures should be available, but a quick glance at the requirements of the Companies Act 1985 will show just how little is available.

The profit margin on sales ratio and the cost ratios that accompany it show how efficiently a company has made and sold its products or services. Also, the size of a firm's profit margin reflects the business that it is in. A high profit margin is usually associated with high-priced goods and services or a business where there is a scarcity factor. A Rolls-Royce has a higher margin than a Ford Escort, and a jeweller's more than a grocer's.

Although the profit margin is very important in a firm's profitability, it is not the only factor, the other being asset utilisation. To illustrate how these two elements tie together, read the story that follows.

A Case to Consider

Here is a summary of the Widebuoy Manufacturing Company's results for the last two years:

	1988	*1989*
	£000	£000
Sales	2 500	3 000
Operating profit	500	600
Assets employed (at year end)	2 000	3 000

At first glance, the business appears to be improving; its sales, operating profit and assets employed all show an increase.

However, calculate the three key ratios and another story emerges:

	1988	*1989*
Profit/sales (%)	20.0	20.0
Sales/assets (times)	1.25	1.0
Profit/assets (%)	25.0	20.0

The profitability of the company has fallen from 25% to 20.0% and a quick glance at the other two ratios tells us why: the profit margin on sales has stayed steady at 20%, but the asset turnover ratio shows a decline from 1.25 times to a mere 1.00 times.

These three ratios are linked together logically and mathematically so that, if you multiply the profit on sales ratio by the asset turnover ratio, you arrive at the profitability ratio:

Profit/sales × sales/assets = Profit/assets

10.5 **How a Business Works**

We can now come to some conclusions about the way any company operates. We have already seen what causes the profit/sales ratio to be high or low and you also *know* when to expect a fast or slow asset turnover ratio.

Which of these sets of ratios belong to:

1 a successful supermarket chain?
2 an unsuccessful heavy engineering company?
3 a jewellery shop?
4 a successful company making electronic equipment?

	Profit/sales	*Sales/assets*	*Profit/assets*
a	20%	1.00	20%
b	4%	4.00	16%
c	7%	0.60	4.2%
d	12%	1.50	18%

The ratios most likely to fit are:

1, b; 2, c; 3, a; 4, d. You may have got **a** and **d** the other way round – the only real clue is that a manufacturer rarely manages to obtain a 20% profit margin and get a reasonable asset turnover as well.

Not every combination of figures is possible, since it is very difficult for a firm to have both a very high profit margin on sales and a very fast turnover of assets at the same time. This is because it is impossible to be simultaneously labour-intensive and capital-intensive. Moreover, a quality product with a high price and with a correspondingly high profit margin is not likely to have the volume of sales to give it a fast turnover of assets. So:

Profit/sales	*and*	*sales/assets*	*Possible?*
high		low	yes
or low		high	yes
or low		low	yes
or high		high	no

Also a high-volume, fast-asset-turnover business can only be a achieved with modest prices – hence supermarkets' very low profit margins.

10.6 Completing the Picture

Sometimes it is necessary to relate the two key factors we have been looking at to the return on equity capital ratio. This is achieved by introducing a gearing ratio into the equation:

$$\frac{\textbf{Net profit after tax}}{\textbf{Sales}} \times \frac{\textbf{Sales}}{\textbf{Assets employed}} \times \frac{\textbf{Assets employed}}{\textbf{Equity capital}} = \frac{\textbf{Net profit after tax}}{\textbf{Equity capital}}$$

A simple example will show that this equation can give you a quick picture of how a company arrived at its return on equity position:

	£million
Sales	24
Net profit after tax	3
Assets employed	20
Equity capital	12
Profit/sales (%)	12.5
Sales/assets	1.2
Gearing	1.67
Profit/equity (%)	25.0

Just how important the gearing part of the equation is, can be seen if you look at the difference between these two sets of ratios:

a 12.0% × 1.00 × 1.10 = 13.2%
b 8.0% × 1.00 × 2.50 = 20.0%

The second differs from the first for two reasons: it has a very high gearing and a lower profit margin on sales. The lower margin is to be expected because its higher gearing implies higher interest payments and so lower profits. But look at the final outcome; much more profitable as far as the shareholders are concerned.

10.7 Summary of Chapters 9 and 10; Limitations of Accounts

Ratio analysis provides the key to interpreting accounting statements. They were grouped into six categories – be sure that you can name them and give some examples of each. There are, of course, other ratios which can be used and the reading list gives you some sources of useful ratios. Be wary of books and articles that quote just a handful of ratios and pretend that nothing else is needed – a great deal more is sought by people who are actually going to invest time or money in a business.

Here is a checklist of the limitations of accounts:

- There is rarely enough detail of costs and results of divisions within large diversified companies.
- The valuation of assets and depreciation can vary from firm to firm, making detailed comparisons risky.
- All the information is history – today's business may be very different.
- The actual definition of terms used may vary from company to company and it is rare for a full definition to be given (e.g. the term 'employee costs' is open to many definitions).
- There is very little in a company's accounts about its prospects. To gain a view of this you have to know about its products, markets, customers and the competition.
- In the end, the success of a company depends on the ability of the people in it, and the accounts rarely give much information about that.

11 Real Company Accounts

In this chapter, the full accounts of a real company (United Biscuits (Holdings) plc) have been reproduced for you to study and evaluate.

In looking at these accounts use the following procedure:

1 Glance at the contents of the report and accounts.
2 Turn to pp. 116–17 and make a note of any increases.
3 Turn to p. 120 and read the directors' report.
4 Read the profit and loss account on pp. 124–5 and the notes that go with it.
5 Read the balance sheets on pp. 126–7 and the notes.
6 Study the source and application of funds statement on pp. 128–9 and make a summary of it in the way we showed (pp. 62 and 63).
7 Analyse the five-year statement on p. 167.
8 Calculate the important ratios (some are already calculated).
9 Read the report again, looking for explanations of any interesting points you have discovered and look for clues as to the firm's prospects.

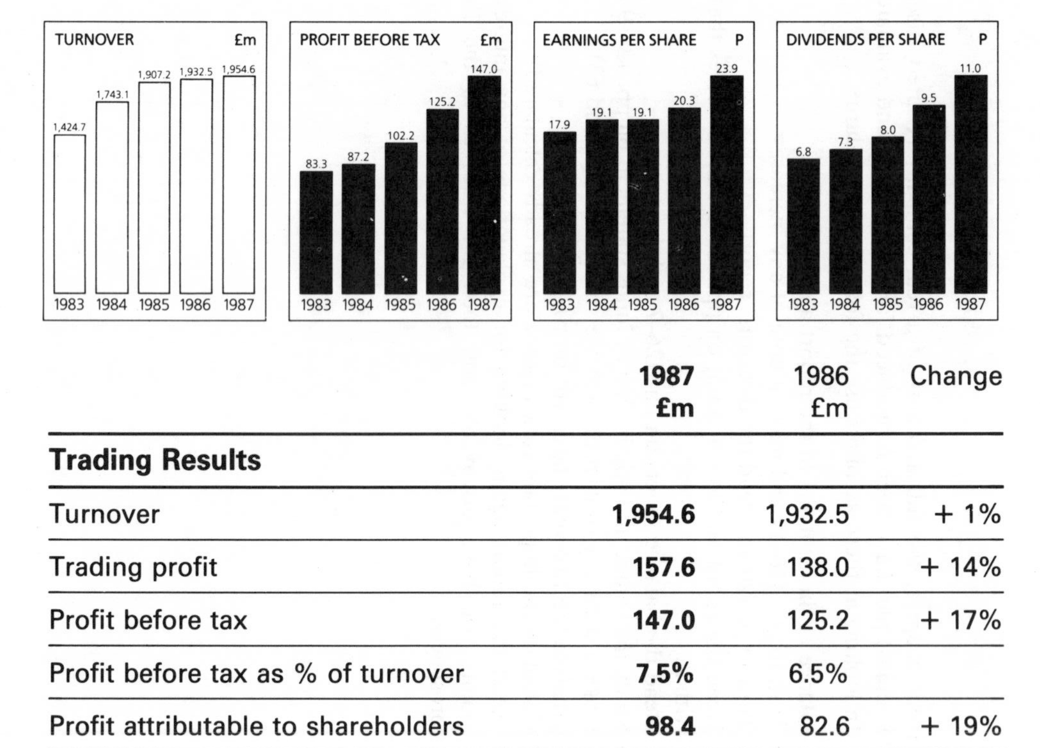

	1987 £m	1986 £m	Change
Trading Results			
Turnover	**1,954.6**	1,932.5	+ 1%
Trading profit	**157.6**	138.0	+ 14%
Profit before tax	**147.0**	125.2	+ 17%
Profit before tax as % of turnover	**7.5%**	6.5%	
Profit attributable to shareholders	**98.4**	82.6	+ 19%

Capital employed			
Average capital employed	**675.7**	639.4	+ 6%
Return on average capital employed	**23%**	22%	
Shareholders' funds at year end	**489.5**	452.9	+ 8%
Capital expenditure	**145.5**	124.7	+ 17%
Per share			
Earnings per share	**23.9p**	20.3p	+ 18%
Dividends per share	**11.0p**	9.5p	+ 16%
Dividend times covered	**2.1**	2.1	
Net assets per share	**118p**	111p	+ 6%

Analysis of Results and Employee Numbers

	Turnover*		Trading Profit		Average number of employees	
	1987	1986	**1987**	1986	**1987**	1986
	£m	£m	**£m**	£m		
UB Foods Europe						
UB Brands	**439.1**	440.2	**58.2**	48.2	**7,111**	7,718
KP Foods	**325.3**	294.3	**36.8**	29.7	**6,391**	6,599
UB Frozen Foods	**108.7**	100.8	**5.3**	3.7	**3,080**	3,083
Pullman Foods†	**6.5**	42.2	**–**	–	**81**	487
Continental Businesses	**77.6**	69.8	**5.5**	4.6	**1,346**	1,320
UB Distribution Services	**36.4**	41.7	**1.8**	1.0	**1,087**	1,312
	993.6	989.0	**107.6**	87.2	**19,096**	20,519
UB Restaurants						
Wimpy	**66.2**	59.6	**7.9**	5.7	**1,848**	1,872
Pizzaland	**58.7**	53.2	**1.1**	4.5	**3,662**	3,500
Overseas	**9.3**	7.6	(0.1)	(0.5)	**760**	535
	134.2	120.4	**8.9**	9.7	**6,270**	5,907
UB Foods US						
Keebler	**679.8**	681.5	**33.4**	32.6	**8,660**	8,251
Specialty Brands	**87.6**	96.5	**11.0**	11.2	**627**	634
	767.4	778.0	**44.4**	43.8	**9,287**	8,885

Other companies						
UK Small Businesses	**85.7**	82.4	**3.4**	2.7	**3,603**	3,551
Shaffer Clarke	**25.2**	23.6	**1.8**	1.9	**58**	50
International	**2.9**	2.6	–	(0.1)	**26**	23
	113.8	108.6	**5.2**	4.5	**3,687**	3,624
Inter-company sales*	**(54.4)**	(63.5)	–	–	–	–
Central overheads	–	–	**(8.5)**	(7.2)	–	–
Central services	–	–	–	–	**954**	1,017
Group	**1,954.6**	1,932.5	**157.6**	138.0	**39,294**	39,952
Geographical analysis						
UK and Ireland	**1,076.2**	1,051.6	**107.1**	89.4		
Continental Europe	**86.9**	77.4	**5.4**	4.2		
USA	**789.2**	801.6	**45.0**	44.4		
Rest of the World	**2.3**	1.9	**0.1**	–		
Group	**1,954.6**	1,932.5	**157.6**	138.0		

*Turnover figures include the invoiced value of goods and services provided to other group divisions and the total of such transactions has been deducted to arrive at group turnover.

†Pullman Foods was sold in March 1987.

Directors' Report

The directors have pleasure in submitting to the members their fortieth annual report together with the audited accounts for the fifty-two weeks ended 2nd January, 1988.

Principal activities
The principal activities of the group are the manufacture and sale of a wide range of food products for both wholesale and retail outlets.

The group's operations during the year and its future prospects are set out in the chairman's and group chief executive's joint statement on pages 2 to 4 and the review of the year on pages 18 to 27.

Turnover and trading profits
A summary of turnover and trading profits is set out on page 28.

Profit and appropriations
The profit and appropriations for the year are as shown in the consolidated profit and loss account on page 32.

An interim dividend of 4.0p per share was paid on 6th January 1988. The directors now recommend a final dividend of 7.0p per share payable on 1st July 1988.

Acquisitions and disposal
On 14th July 1987 a 30 per cent shareholding in Industria Confezioni Alimentari Spa, an Italian crisp and snack manufacturer, was acquired for a cash consideration of £4.1m. During 1987 a further investment of £1.6 was made in Aguia SA, a Brazilian biscuit manufacturer, taking the group's investment at the year end to 39 per cent.

products and in more efficient and effective production and packaging machinery.

Employee share schemes
Eligible employees were invited in June 1987 to apply for options over the ordinary shares of the company in terms of the company's 1981 savings-related share option scheme. Options over 1,419,631 shares were granted at a subscription price of 282p per share which will normally be exercisable in the six months following the maturing of the relevant five year SAYE contract.

On 13th April 1987 options over 602,637 shares were granted in terms of the 1984 executive share option scheme to directors and nominated executives at a subscription price of 266p per share. On 21st September 1987 options over a further 133,106 shares were granted at a subscription price of 322p per share.
These options will be exercisable between three and ten years from the date of grant.

On 7th May, 1987 shareholders approved the adoption of a profit sharing scheme which has since been approved by the inland Revenue under the provisions of the Finance Act 1978. The scheme permits the directors to allocate to trustees profits in any financial year up to a maximum of five per cent of the consolidated pre-tax profit attributable to the United Kingdom activities of the group. The directors have decided to allocate to the trustees the sum of £1.2m in respect of the year under review to enable them to subscribe for new shares in the company on behalf of eligible employees.

Emloyment policies
The group has a comprehensive framework of employment policies, some of which apply throughout the group, with others appropriate to the

On 16th March 1987 Pullman Foods, a national wholesale distributor of frozen foods, was sold to Fitch Lovell plc for a consideration of £5.8m.

Land and buildings
The directors are of the opinion that any differences between current market valuations and book values of land and buildings in the group are not material.

Post balance sheet events
It was announced on 12th January 1988 that agreement had been reached in principle for the sale of Specialty Brands. The refrigerated salad dressings and olive businesses are to be acquired by Campbell Soup Company and, subject to the requirements of the Federal Trade Commission, the spices, herbs and vinegar businesses are to be acquired by McCormick & Company, Inc. The net proceeds of the sale after tax and expenses are expected to be $170m (equivalent to £90m at current exchange rates).

On 16th March 1988 it was announced that United Biscuits had conditionally agreed to acquire Ross Young's, which formed a major part of the food division of Imperial Group plc, from Hanson plc for an acquisition consideration of £335m. A circular was issued to shareholders on 18th March 1988 giving full details of the proposed acquisition, the method of financing and the estimated effect on the group balance sheet. An extraordinary general meeting has been convened for 12th April 1988 when shareholders will be asked to approve the acquisition.

Research and development
The group has maintained its commitment to research and development. Continuity of investment in this area is essential if the group is to retain a competitive position in the development of new particular subsidiary or part of the business concerned.

It is group policy that employees at all levels shall not in the course of employment discriminate against any other person, or be discriminated against on the grounds of colour, race, religion, sex, marital status, or ethnic or national origins. This policy applies in respect of all conditions of work, including salaries and wages, hours of work, holiday entitlement, overtime and shift work, work allocation, sick pay, recruitment, training, promotion, redundancy and use of available amenities.

It is the group's policy to offer equal opportunity to disabled persons, whether registered or not, applying for vacancies having regard to their aptitudes and abilities. Arrangements are made to continue the employment of those employees who have become disabled persons during the course of their employment with the group whenever possible. Consideration is also given for arranging appropriate training facilities or providing special aids where necessary.

The group's policy is to provide disabled persons with the same opportunities for training, career development and promotion that are available to all employees within the limitations of their aptitudes and abilities.
There are regular consultations at all levels with employees through union representatives, staff councils, consultative committees and at conferences, on matters likely to affect employees' interests. The chairman and directors regularly visit locations throught the group to talk to an consult with employees at all levels. Information on matters of concern to employees is given through employee reports, covering group and subsidiaries, in-house newspapers and other publications.

The group has operated a savings-related share option scheme for UK employees since 1974 and is offering an initial participation in the profit sharing scheme approved by shareholders last year.

It is the group's policy not only to comply with the safety and health measures required bny law, but to act positively to ensure that its premises are safe and healthy places in which to work. It recognises that the health, safety and welfare of all its employees, whether on group premises or carrying out group business elsewhere, is primarily the management's responsibility.

In addition, the group recognises it has a responsibility for the health and safety of other persons whilst they are on our premises.

The group recognises the need for a well trained and adaptable work force at all levels. To this end substantial resources are directed to training and development, and training activities are continuously up-dated and enhanced.

Charitable and political contributions
During the year the total of charitable donations made by the group in the United Kingdom amounted to £415,000. Political contributions to the Conservative Party amounted to £100,000.

Share capital
During the year 8,003,706 ordinary shares were issued as a result of the exercise of options and warrants. Since the year end a further 1,574,842 shares have been issued in respect of the exercise of options and warrants.

Authority was given to the directors at the annual general meeting in 1985 to allot all of the company's authorised but unissued shares. This authority is due to expire in May 1990. The power given to the and Lord Plumb. Mr Bondy, who reached the age of 67 in December 1987, does not offer himself for re-election. He has been a non-executive director since 1982 and the directors wish to record their appreciation of the major contribution which he has made to the group's affairs during his period of office.

Sir Hector Laing, Sir James Cleminson and Lord Plumb, being eligible, offer themselves for re-election.

Sir Hector Laing's service agreement with the company expires on 31st May 1990, at which time he will be aged 67. Sire Hector has spent his entire working life with United Biscuits, having joinded the board of McVitiel & Price in 1945. He has been group chairman since 1972 and was chief executive from 1964 to 1986.
His fellow directors have resolved that, in recognition of his contribution to the development and growth of United Biscuits, his pension benefits on retirement should be augmented within limits set by the Inland Revenue. They have further resolved that the cost of augmentation should be funded by three annual instalments of £170,000 into a group pension scheme.
The first of thise payments was made in December 1987 and is included in emoluments as executives reported in note 25 to the accounts on page 48.

Sir James Cleminson and Lord Plumb as non-executive directors do not have service contracts.

Executive directors of the company are eligible to be granted options under the company's share option schemes. No other arrangements to which the company was a party subsisted at the end of the year or at any time during the year which would directors at the annual general meeting in 1987 to permit the directors to issue equity securities for cash, subject to certain limits, without first offering them pro rata to exisiting shareholders is due to expire at this year's annual general meeting.

At the time of signing this report it is not known whether the authorised share capital of the company will be increased pursuant to the resolution to be proposed at the extraordinary general meeting to be held on 12th April 1988 in connection with the acquisition of Ross Young's Holdings Limited. If it is so increased the directors will, by virtue of the same resolution, also have been given power to issue equity securities for cash, subject to certain limits, without first offering them to existing shareholders until the annual general meeting. There is included in the notice of annual general meeting, notice of a special resolution to give power to the directors until the annual general meeting in 1989 to issue equity securities up to five per cent of the issued share capital of the company as at the end of 1987 to third parties for cash without first offering them to existing shareholders or, in connection with a rights issue, where the equity securities respectively attributable to the interests of all shareholders are proportionate (as nearly as may be) to the respective numbers of shares held by them.

Directors
The names of the directors of the company and their biographical details are set out on pages 6 and 7.

F W Knight and D R J Stewart were appointed directors on 4th February 1987 and were re-elected at the annual general meeting on 7th May 1987.

The directors who retire by rotation this year are Sir Hector Laing, E L Bondy Jnr, Sir James Cleminson enable directors or their families to acquire benefits by the acquisition of shares in, or debentures of, the company or any other body corporate.

No director had, during the year or at the end of the year, any material interest in any contract of significance to the group's business.

Interests in the share capital of the company
So far as is known, no person holds or is benefically interested in more than five per cent of the share capital.

The interests of the directors and their families in the share capital of the company at the beginning and end of the year, or at the date of appointment if later, are set out in note 24 to the accounts. There have been no changes in these interests between 2nd January and 30th March 1988.

Status of the company
The company is not a close company within the meaning of the Income and Corporation Taxes Act 1970.

Auditors
A resolution to reappoint Deloitte Haskins & Sells and Arthur Young as joint auditors of the company will be put to the annual general meeting.

On behalf of the board

D R J Stewart
Secretary

30th March 1988

Consolidated Profit and Loss Account

for the 52 weeks ended 2nd January 1988

Notes		**1987 52 weeks £m**	1986 53 weeks £m
	Turnover	**1,954.6**	1,932.5
	Trade discounts	**122.2**	114.1
	Turnover after trade discounts	**1,832.4**	1,818.4
	Cost of sales	**1,040.9**	1,054.1
	Gross profit	**791.5**	764.3
	Distribution, selling and marketing costs	**514.4**	518.3
	Administrative expenses	**121.4**	109.4
	Other income	**(1.9)**	(1.4)
3	**Trading profit**	**157.6**	138.0
4	Interest	**9.4**	12.8
	Profit before profit sharing	**148.2**	125.2
5	Profit sharing	**1.2**	–

Note			
	Profit on ordinary activities before tax	**147.0**	125.2
6	Tax on profit on ordinary activities	**48.3**	42.5
	Profit on ordinary activities after tax	**98.7**	82.7
	Minority interests	**0.3**	0.1
	Profit attributable to shareholders	**98.4**	82.6
7	Extraordinary charges	**7.9**	6.8
	Profit for the financial year	**90.5**	75.8
8	Dividends	**46.2**	38.8
20	**Balance to reserves**	**44.3**	37.0
9	**Earnings per share**	**23.9p**	20.3p

Consolidated Balance Sheet
2nd January 1988

Notes		**1987**	1986
		£m	£m
	Fixed assets		
10	Tangible assets	**557.2**	536.1
12	Investments	**7.2**	2.5
		564.4	538.6
	Current assets		
13	Stocks	**143.0**	152.5
14	Debtors	**214.5**	210.5
15	Taxation	**0.9**	1.9
	Short-term deposits and loans	**89.6**	139.8
	Cash at bank and in hand	**39.9**	38.1
		487.9	542.8
	Creditors: amounts falling due within one year		
16	Trade and other creditors	**253.5**	266.0
17	Loans, overdrafts and finance lease obligations	**35.9**	42.0
	Taxation	**41.1**	26.0
	Dividends	**46.0**	38.8
		376.5	372.8

Note			
	Net current assets	**111.4**	170.0
	Total assets less current liabilities	**675.8**	708.6
	Creditors: amounts falling due after more than one year		
17	Loans and finance lease obligations	**154.7**	231.2
	Taxation	**21.3**	13.8
18	**Provisions for liabilities and charges**	**9.3**	10.0
		185.3	255.0
		490.5	453.6
	Capital and reserves		
19	Called up share capital	**104.0**	102.0
20	Share premium account	**130.5**	121.1
20	Revaluation and other reserves	**15.4**	15.9
20	Profit and loss account	**239.6**	213.9
		489.5	452.9
	Minority interests	**1.0**	0.7
		490.5	453.6

Signed on behalf of the board on 30th March 1988

Hector Laing

James Blyth

Consolidated Statement of Source and Application of Funds

for the 52 weeks ended 2nd January 1988

Notes		**1987 52 weeks £m**	1986 53 weeks £m
	Source of funds		
	Profit on ordinary activities before tax	**147.0**	125.2
	Adjustment for item not involving the movement of funds Depreciation	**55.9**	52.8
	Total generated from operations	**202.9**	178.0
	Funds from other sources		
	Proceeds of share issues	**11.4**	1.4
	Disposal of fixed assets	**19.9**	13.3
	Loans drawn down	**46.1**	58.9
22	Disposal of Pullman Foods	**4.7**	–
	Surplus arising from Imperial Group plc offers	–	4.9
23	Decrease in working capital	–	43.9
		82.1	122.4

Note			
	Application of funds		
	Dividends paid	**39.0**	32.5
	Purchase of fixed assets	**145.4**	124.1
	Purchase of investments	**7.4**	0.3
	Tax paid	**29.6**	25.0
	Loans repaid or becoming repayable within one year	**88.6**	24.6
	Exchange differences	**8.4**	0.4
	Expenditure against provisions	**3.1**	22.4
22	Acquisition of business	–	1.2
23	Increase in working capital	**5.8**	–
		327.3	230.5
	(Decrease)/increase in net liquid funds	**(42.3)**	69.9
	Movement in net liquid funds		
	Bank balances, cash and deposits	**(48.4)**	90.8
	Overdrafts and loans payable within one year	**6.1**	(20.9)
		(42.3)	69.9

Exchange adjustments on working capital and net liquid funds are included in the respective movements.

Company Balance Sheet
2nd January 1988

Notes		**1987** **£m**	1986 £m
	Fixed assets		
	Investments		
11	Investment in subsidiaries	**359.2**	355.2
12	Trade investments	**0.1**	0.1
		359.3	355.3
	Current assets		
14	Debtors	**0.2**	0.1
15	Taxation	**11.0**	15.0
	Short-term deposits	–	0.7
		11.2	15.8
	Creditors: amounts falling due within one year		
16	Trade and other creditors	**0.1**	0.1
17	Loans and overdrafts	**10.7**	8.5
	Taxation	**11.4**	15.3
	Dividends	**46.0**	38.8
		68.2	62.7

Note			
	Net current liabilities	**(57.0)**	(46.9)
	Total assets less current liabilities	**302.3**	308.4
	Creditors: amounts falling due after more than one year		
17	Loans	**9.0**	10.5
18	**Provisions for liabilities and charges**	**5.8**	5.8
		14.8	16.3
		287.5	292.1
	Capital and reserves		
19	Called up share capital	**104.0**	102.0
20	Share premium account	**130.5**	121.1
20	Revaluation and other reserves	**42.7**	42.7
20	Profit and loss account	**10.3**	26.3
		287.5	292.1

Signed on behalf of the board on 30th March 1988

Hector Laing

James Blyth

1 Accounting policies

Basis of accounting
The accounts are prepared on the historical cost basis of accounting, except for the revaluation of certain assets.

Basis of consolidation
The group accounts consolidate the accounts of the company and all of its subsidiaries. The results of businesses acquired during the year are included in the profit and loss account from their dates of acquisition; the results of businesses disposed of during the year are included in the profit and loss account up to their dates of disposal. Principal subsidiaries are listed in note 11.

No profit and loss account is presented for United Biscuits (Holdings) plc as provided by Section 228 (7) of the Companies Act 1985.

Comparative figures
Certain comparative figures in the accounts and the notes thereto have been revised in minor respects onto a basis consistent with that applied in the current year.

Turnover
Turnover consists of sales to third parties before discounts and excludes value added tax.

Goodwill
Goodwill arising on the acquisition of both incorporated and unincorporated businesses is computed on the basis of fair value of assets

Commodity purchases
Certain commodities are purchased on the futures markets in order to minimise the cost of ingredients. When Contracts are closed, the realised surpluses and deficits are applied against the cost of the related ingredients in the year of delivery.

Pensions
Pensions relating to current and past service are funded by way of annual contributions to pension plans. The amounts of such contributions are determined following consultation with independent actuaries.

Pension costs are accounted for as follows:

(i) Contributions in respect of current service, amortisation of past service liabilities (other than those described in (ii) below) and notional interest on unfunded past service liabilities, are charged annually against trading profit.

(ii) The present value of future contributions relating to unfunded past service liabilities is either accrued and charged to the profit and loss account as an extraordinary item at the time of inception of a pension plan, or where appropriate, accrued by way of adjustment to goodwill at the date of acquisition of a subsidiary.

acquired. Goodwill is charged to reserves as it arises.

Tangible assets
Depreciation is calculated to write off the cost or valuation of the assets (net of government grants) over their expected useful lives by equal annual instalments principally at the following rates:

Land and buildings (except as noted below) – $1\frac{1}{2}$% unless
short leasehold.
short leaseholds – over the life of the lease.
Plant – 3-15%.
Vehicles – 20-30%.

Revalued buildings are depreciated over their remaining useful lives as estimated at revaluation date.

Leasing and hire purchase commitments
Assets obtained under finance leases and hire purchase contracts are capitalised in the balance sheet and are depreciated over their useful lives. The interest element of the rental obligations is charged to profit and loss account over the period of the primary lease and represents a constant proportion of the balance of capital repayments outstanding. Rentals paid under operating leases are charged to income on a straight line basis over the term of the lease.

Stocks
Stocks are valued at the lower of cost and net realisable value. Cost in the case of products manufactured by the group comprises direct material and labour cost together with appropriate factory overheads.

Taxation
Deferred taxation is provided on all timing differences of material amount except where no liability is likely to arise in the foreseeable future. Advance corporation tax is carried forward provided that it is expected to be offset against corporation tax liabilities on the profits of the next accounting period.

Foreign currency translations

Company
Monetary assets and liabilities denominated in foreign currencies are translated at the rate of exchange rulilng at the balance sheet date. Transactions in foreign currencies are recorded at the rate ruling at the date of the transaction, all differences being taken to the profit and loss account.

Group
The profit and loss accounts of overseas subsidiaries are translated at a weighted average rate of exchange, and the balance sheets are translated at the rate of exchange ruling at the year end. The exchange differences arising are taken directly to reserves. All other translation differences are taken to the profit and loss account with the exception of differences on foreign currency borrowings to the extent that they are used to finance or provide a hedge against group equity investments in foreign enterprises. These are taken directly to reserves together with the exchange difference on the net assets of the related investments.

2 Segmental information

The group's turnover, trading profit and average number of employees are analysed on page 28.

3 Trading profit

Trading profit is after charging:

	1987	1986
	£m	£m
Depreciation	**55.9**	52.8
Operating lease rentals – plant and machinery	**13.4**	13.6
– land and buildings	**19.2**	17.5
Directors' emoluments (see note 25)	**2.1**	1.5

The auditors' remuneration amounted to £849,000 (1986 £812,000).

4 Interest

	1987	1986
	£m	£m
Interest payable		
Bank loans and overdrafts	**1.6**	1.7
Loans wholly repayable within five years	**5.1**	7.7
Loans not wholly repayable within five years	**8.8**	10.2
Lease and other	**3.3**	2.5
	18.8	22.1

	1987	1986
Interest receivable		
Short-term deposits and loans	**7.5**	8.0
Other	**1.9**	1.3
	9.4	9.3
	9.4	12.8

5 Profit sharing

	1987 £m	1986 £m
Allocation of profit in respect of the 1987 group employee profit sharing scheme approved by the Inland Revenue under the provisions of the Finance Act 1978	**1.2**	–

6 Tax on profit on ordinary activities

	1987 £m	1986 £m
On the profit for the year		
UK corporation tax at 35% (1986 36.25%)	**72.0**	25.9
Relief for overseas taxation	**34.4**	–

	1987	1986
	37.6	25.9
Overseas corporation taxes	**14.3**	4.6
Deferred tax	**(1.6)**	11.0
Adjustments in respect of prior years	**(2.0)**	1.0
	48.3	42.5

The tax charge for the year has been reduced by £4.6m (1986 £5.7m) in respect of capital allowances and other timing differences.

7 Extraordinary charges

	1987	1986
	£m	£m
Effect of US Tax Reform Act of 1986 on taxation liabilities	**6.6**	–
Other items	**1.3**	6.8
	7.9	6.8

8 Dividends

	1987	1986
	£m	£m
Payable – interim 4.0p per share (1986 3.5p)	**16.6**	14.3
Proposed – final 7.0p per share (1986 6.0p)	**29.4**	24.5
Underprovision in respect of prior year	**0.2**	–
	46.2	38.8

9 Earnings per share

The calculation of earnings per share is based upon the weighted average number of shares in issue during the year – 412.2m (1986 407.3m) – and profit attributable to shareholders. Earnings per share on a fully diluted basis is not materially different from that calculated below.

	1987	1986
	£m	£m
Profit attributable to shareholders	**98.4**	82.6
Earnings per share	**23.9p**	20.3p

10 Tangible assets

	Land & buildings Freehold	Leasehold	Plant, machinery & vehicles	Fixtures & fittings	Projects in progress	Total
	£m	£m	£m	£m	£m	£m
Cost – less government grants – or valuation						
At 3rd January 1987	147.0	57.2	428.9	71.5	53.1	757.7
Exchange adjustment	(12.6)	(1.6)	(44.0)	(2.2)	(4.1)	(64.5)
Additions	4.3	5.7	49.3	19.4	66.8	145.5
Government grants	(0.1)	–	–	–	–	(0.1)
Disposals	(3.3)	(5.7)	(33.4)	(8.5)	(0.4)	(51.3)
Reclassifications	11.6	1.3	32.1	1.8	(46.8)	–

At 2nd January 1988	146.9	56.9	432.9	82.0	68.6	787.3
Depreciation						
At 3rd January 1987	17.4	11.8	168.3	24.1	–	221.6
Exchange adjustment	(1.5)	(0.5)	(16.2)	(1.0)	–	(19.2)
Charge for year	4.4	2.2	38.1	11.2	–	55.9
Disposals	(0.6)	(1.3)	(21.7)	(4.6)	–	(28.2)
Reclassifications	(0.3)	–	–	0.3	–	–
At 2nd January 1988	19.4	12.2	168.5	30.0	–	230.1
Net book value at 2nd January 1988	127.5	44.7	264.4	52.0	68.6	557.2
Net book value at 3rd January 1987	129.6	45.4	260.6	47.4	53.1	536.1

The net book value of leasehold properties includes £35.9m (1986 £36.5m) in respect of leases with under fifty years to run at 2nd January 1988.

An analysis of the net book value of land and buildings included at valuation is provided below together with an analysis of the value of such assets determined according to the historical cost accounting rules.

Net book value of land and buildings included at valuation

	At 2nd January 1988		At 3rd January 1987	
	Freehold	Leasehold	Freehold	Leasehold
	£m	£m	£m	£m
At valuation 1980	35.8	3.4	36.6	3.5
At valuation 1981	25.8	3.6	33.0	4.6
At valuation 1983	0.3	–	0.4	–
	61.9	7.0	70.0	8.1

Historical cost equivalent of land and buildings at valuation

	At 2nd January 1988		At 3rd January 1987	
	Freehold	Leasehold	Freehold	Leasehold
	£m	£m	£m	£m
Historical cost	66.2	6.6	75.2	7.5
Depreciation based on historical cost	13.6	2.9	13.7	3.0
Net book value	52.6	3.7	61.5	4.5

The assets of businesses acquired by the group are reflected in the consolidated accounts at their fair value as at acquisition date. These fair values represent the historical costs of the relevant assets to the group; accordingly, such assets are excluded from the analysis above (unless subject to revaluation since acquisition).

No provision has been made for tax which might become payable if any revalued properties were disposed of for their revalued amounts in view of their continuing use by the group.

Analysis of leased tangible assets

The book value of tangible assets acquired under finance lease arrangements included on page 38 is set out below:

	Land & buildings	Plant, machinery, etc.	Total
	£m	£m	£m
At 2nd January 1988			
Cost	6.6	15.0	21.6
Depreciation	6.4	6.4	8.8
Net book value	4.2	8.6	12.8
Net book value at 3rd January 1987	5.5	5.0	10.5

11 Investment in subsidiaries

	1987	1987
	£m	£m
Shares in subsidiaries (see below)	**99.4**	146.8
Due from subsidiaries	**228.8**	214.1
Dividends receivable from subsidiaries	**31.1**	–

	359.2	360.9
Due to subsidiary	–	5.7
	359.2	355.2

The amounts due from subsidiaries and the amount due to a subsidiary are payable on demand. There is no present intention that such payments will be made within the next year.

Shares in subsidiaries at cost

	£m
At 3rd January 1987	146.8
Transfers to subsidiaries	(47.4)
At 2nd January 1988	99.4

Principal subsidiaries	**Activities**	**Country of incorporation and operation**
UB Investments plc	Holding company	UK*
United Biscuits (UK) Limited	Food manufacturer and processor	UK*
Cochranes Vehicle Holdings Limited (51%)	Motor vehicle distributor	UK*
Keebler Company	Food manufacturer	USA
Specialty Brands Inc.	Salad dressing, spices & olives processor	USA

Shaffer, Clarke & Co. Inc.	Food marketer	USA
UB Finance BV	Finance company	Netherlands
NV Westimex (Belgium) SA	Snack manufacturer	Belgium
Productos Ortiz SA	Food manufacturer	Spain

*Registered in Scotland

As at 2nd January 1988, all the above subsidiaries were wholy owned except for Cochranes Vehicle Holdings Limited and were held through other subsidiaries with the exception of UB Investments plc and Cochranes Vehicle Holdings Limited. The group also held investments in other subsidiaries which were either not trading or not significant. In compliance with the Companies Act 1985, details of all subsidiaries will be annexed to the company's next annual return.

12 Investments

	Group			Company
	Associated companies	Trade & other investments	Total	Trade investments
	£m	£m	£m	£m
Cost less goodwill				
At 3rd January 1987	0.3	1.3	1.6	0.1
Additions	5.2	2.2	7.4	–

Transfer	0.4	(0.4)	–	–
Goodwill	(2.8)	–	(2.8)	–
At 2nd January, 1988	3.1	3.1	6.2	0.1
Post-acquisition reserves				
At 3rd January 1987	0.9	–	0.9	–
Exchange adjustment	(0.1)	–	(0.1)	–
Retained	0.2	–	0.2	–
At 2nd January 1988	1.0	–	1.0	–
Netbook value at 2nd January 1988	4.1	3.1	7.2	0.1
Netbook value at 3rd January 1987	1.2	1.3	2.5	0.1

The group's trade investments include listed investments at cost £0.5m (1986 £0.5m) with a market value at 2nd January 1988 of £2.4m (1986 £2.1m).

Name of company	Country of registration (or incorporation) and operation	Holding	Proportion held	Activities
Associated companies				
Aguia SA	Brazil	Ordinary shares	38.8%	Biscuit manufacturer
Industria Confezioni Alimentari Spa	Italy	Ordinary shares	30%	Snack manufacturer & distributer
Meiji McVitie Limited	Japan	Common stock	50%	Biscuit marketer
CFC McVitie Inc	Philippines	Ordinary shares	40%	Biscuit manufacturer
Unlisted trade investments				
Jas. Bowman & Sons Limited	England	Ordinary shares	14.8%	Flour miller
Clark & Butcher Limited	England	Preference shares	100%	Flour miller

13 Stocks

	1987	1986
	£m	£m
Raw materials and consumables	**60.1**	66.5
Work in progress	**3.1**	2.7
Finished goods	**79.8**	83.3
	143.0	152.5

There is no material difference between the replacement cost and historical cost of stocks.

14 Debtors

	Group		Company	
	1987	1986	**1987**	1986
	£m	£m	**£m**	£m
Trade debtors	**185.4**	178.8	**0.1**	0.1
Associated companies	**1.2**	1.7	**–**	–
Other debtors	**8.2**	8.9	**–**	–
Prepayments and accrued income	**19.7**	21.1	**0.1**	–
	214.5	210.5	**0.2**	0.1

Debtors include £2.4m (1986 £3.5m) which is not due within one year.

15 Taxation

	Group				Company
	Advance corporation tax	Other timing differences	Accelerated capital allowances	Total	Advance corporation tax
	£m	£m	£m	£m	£m
At 3rd January 1987	15.0	(5.1)	(8.0)	1.9	15.0

Profit and loss charge	—	(1.8)	3.4	1.6	–
1987 extraordinary item	–	(0.2)	–	(0.2)	–
Movement in year	(4.0)	–	–	(4.0)	(4.0)
Exchange differences	–	1.6	–	1.6	–
At 2nd January 1988	11.0	(5.5)	(4.6)	0.9	11.0

The whole amount of the tax asset, both group and company, is recoverable after more than one year from the balance sheet date.

The group's potential liabilities for deferred taxation which have not been provided for in the accounts are as follows:

	1987	1986
	£m	£m
Accelerated capital allowances	**82.0**	85.1
Revaluation of properties	**3.8**	3.9
Other timing differences	**(7.5)**	(8.6)
	78.3	80.4

No provision has been made for taxation that would arise in the event of certain overseas subsidiaries and associated companies distributing their reserves.

16 Trade and other creditors

	Group		Company	
	1987	1986	**1987**	1986
	£m	£m	**£m**	£m
Trade creditors	**82.9**	88.3	**–**	–
Associated companies	**–**	0.1	**–**	–
Other creditors	**55.6**	56.0	**–**	–
Accruals and deferred income	**115.0**	121.6	**0.1**	0.1
	253.5	266.0	**0.1**	0.1

Other creditors include £30.0m (1986 £33.7m) payable to central and local governments in respect of VAT and other sales taxes, social security and other payroll deductions, and miscellaneous taxes. Other creditors also include £3.9m (1986 £2.9m) which is not due within one year from the balance sheet date.

17 Loans, overdrafts and finance lease obligations

	Group		Company	
	1987 £m	1986 £m	**1987 £m**	1986 £m
Bank loans and overdrafts				
Bank loans	**9.1**	9.7	–	–
Overdrafts	**28.9**	15.1	**10.7**	8.5
	38.0	24.8	**10.7**	8.5
Debenture and other loans				
8% debenture stock 1993/98 (secured)	**9.0**	9.0	**9.0**	9.0
$5\frac{1}{4}$% unsecured loan stock 2003/08	–	1.5	–	1.5
$8\frac{7}{8}$% £25m guaranteed bonds 1989	**25.0**	25.0	–	–
9% US $23.7m guaranteed bonds 1989	–	15.9	–	–
11% US $50m guaranteed bonds 1990	–	33.5	–	–
$6\frac{1}{2}$% US $75m guaranteed bonds 1996	**39.9**	50.3	–	–
US $ Euronotes	**24.0**	63.7	–	–
$8\frac{3}{4}$%-$9\frac{7}{8}$% mortgages and other secured bonds 2001/2003	**1.1**	1.9	–	–
$8\frac{1}{2}$% US $16.9m senior notes 1997	**9.0**	12.4	–	–
8.7% US $25m senior notes 2002	**13.3**	–	–	–
11.54% US $12.5m senior notes 1999	**6.7**	8.4	–	–
6%-$12\frac{1}{2}$% equipment purchase obligations 1995/2008	**10.1**	12.8	–	–

	138.1	234.4	**9.0**	10.5
Finance lease obligations	**14.5**	14.0	–	–
	190.6	273.2	**19.7**	19.0
Repayable as follows:				
Over five years – by instalment	**64.3**	66.4	–	–
– other	**48.9**	61.3	**9.0**	10.5
	113.2	127.7	**9.0**	10.5
Over two years and under five years	**9.7**	91.4	–	–
Over one year and under two years	**31.8**	12.1	–	–
	154.7	231.2	**9.0**	10.5
Under one year	**35.9**	42.0	**10.7**	8.5
	190.6	273.2	**19.7**	19.0

Notes:

1. The debenture stock is repayable at par and is secured by a floating charge over certain UK assets.
2. The $5\frac{1}{4}$% unsecured loan stock was redeemed at 80% on 7th April 1987.
3. The $8\frac{7}{8}$% guaranteed bonds are redeemable at par in 1989.

4. The 9% guaranteed bonds were redeemed at 100.5% on 5th February 1987.

5. The 11% guaranteed bonds were redeemed in the year, \$5.0m at par on 23rd July 1987, \$2.3m at 101.375% on 21st July 1987 and \$42.7m at 101.5% on 28th August 1987.

6. The $6\frac{1}{2}$% guaranteed bonds are redeemable at par in 1996.

7. The Euronotes are short-term borrowings representing part of a multi-option facility of US \$120m available to the group until 1993. Euronotes \$95m were outstanding on 3rd January 1987 and \$45m on 2nd January 1988. It is the group's intention to continue issuing notes within the foreseeable future and consequently they are included as part of long-term debt.

8. The $8\frac{1}{2}$% senior notes are repayable by annual instalments of \$1.6m with a final payment of \$2.3m in 1997.

9. The 8.7% senior notes are repayable by annual instalments of \$2.5m from 1993.

10. The 11.54% senior notes are repayable by annual instalments of \$1.25m beginning in 1989.

11. The equipment purchase obligations include £1.3m (1986 £1.7m) which are secured on specific assets of the group.

12. The amount of bank loans repayable after more than five years is £1.3m (1986 £0.3m); in more than two and less than five years £2.3m (1986

£3.8m); and in more than one year and less than two years £3.4m (1986 £2.6m). The amount of current bank loans is £2.1m (1986 £3.0m).

13. The total amount of loans repayable by instalment with at least one instalment not due for more than five years was £76.2m (1986 £98.1m) which amount includes £1.3m (1986 £0.3m) in respect of bank loans.

14. The finance lease obligations are generally secured on the tangible assets to which the obligations relate (see note 10).

18 Provisions for liabilities and charges

	Group			Company
	Deferred liabilities for pensions	Extra-ordinary provisions	Total	Provision for losses of subsidiary
	£m	£m	£m	£m
As at 3rd January 1987	7.8	2.2	10.0	5.8
Exchange adjustment	(1.2)	–	(1.2)	–
Profit and loss charge	1.1	–	1.1	–
Amounts paid or becoming current	(0.5)	(0.1)	(0.6)	–
As at 2nd January 1988	7.2	2.1	9.3	5.8

Deferred liabilities for pensions

Under its pension schemes, the group has undertaken to make annual payments to fund certain past service liabilities. The years in which the annual payments cease and their estimated present value are as follows:

	1987	1986
	£m	£m
1993	**1.0**	1.1
1996	**1.7**	2.4
2000	**1.2**	1.3
Other	**3.8**	3.6
	7.7	8.4
Current portion	**(0.5)**	(0.6)
	7.2	7.8

Pension commitments

The group remains intent on making such annual contribution to its pension schemes as are considered appropriate following consultation with independent actuaries.

In the case of the UK pension schemes, which cover the majority of UK employees, the most recent actuarial valuations at 1st June 1985 indicated that current contribution rates were adequate to meet the future liabilities of these schemes.

In the case of Keebler's pension scheme, the annual company contribution includes amortisation of past service costs over twenty years; a proportion of these past service costs is provided for in the consolidated balance sheet within deferred liabilities for pensions. Keebler also contributes to various multi-employer union pension schemes, and can be liable for funding those schemes' actuarial deficits if it withdraws therefrom. Keebler has no intention to withdraw from these schemes.

19 Share capital

	£m
Ordinary shares of 25p each	
Authorised 547.0 million shares (1986 547.0 million)	136.8
Allotted, called up and fully paid at 3rd January 1987 – 407.9 million shares	102.0
Shares issued – 1.8 million under company share option schemes	0.5
– 6.2 million on exercise of 1989 warrants	1.5
Allotted, called up and fully paid 2nd January 1988 – 415.9 million shares	104.0

Warrants

In terms of a deed poll dated 18th April 1984 the company issued 17.5 million warrants to subscribe for 17.5 million ordinary shares at 155p per share in the period up to 31st March 1989. As a result of the 1985 rights issue the number of shares for which warrant holders may subscribe has been increased to 18.2 million at an adjusted subscription price of 149p per share. There were 11.6m warrants outstanding at the year end.

In terms of a deed poll dated 25th June 1986 the company issued 20.3 million warrants to subscribe for 20.3 million ordinary shares at 247p per share in the period up to 25th June 1991.

Employee share schemes

The company has three share option schemes: the 1974 share option scheme, the 1981 share option scheme and the 1984 executive share option scheme. All schemes have been approved by UB shareholders and the 1981 share option scheme and the 1984 executive share option scheme have been approved by the Board of Inland Revenue.

A total of 50 million shares has been allocated for issue to employees under the company's share option schemes. At 2nd January 1988, 10.8 million shares had been issued and options over a further 9.3 million shares were outstanding, leaving a balance of 29.9 million shares over which options may be granted by not later than May 1990.

The subscription prices for each year, shares issued during the year and shares under option at 2nd January 1988 are set out below:

	Subscription price per share	Shares issued during the year	Shares under option outstanding at the end of the year
a)Savings-related			
1979	77p	52,504	–
1980	77p	44,836	48,588
1981	$102\frac{1}{2}$p	17,262	–
1982	$100\frac{1}{2}$p	500,222	35,815
1983	$125\frac{1}{2}$p	16,297	429,093
1984	$128\frac{1}{2}$p/143p	25,358	1,252,890
1985	159p	2,309	386,576
1986	218	1,356	606,429
1987	282p	–	1,394,738
b)Executive			
1981	111p	264,592	–
1982	$118\frac{1}{2}$p	57,131	–
1983	139p	72,580	315,320
1983	133p	190,160	1,174,381
1984	$156\frac{1}{2}$p	356,320	984,012
1984 (Parallel)	152p	243,944	
1985 (April)	190p	–	786,862
1985 (Sept)	173p	–	615,095
1986 (May)	245p	–	549,311
1986 (Sept)	230p	–	30,478

1987 (April)	266p	–	602,637
1987 (Sept)	322p	–	133,106
Shares issued during the year and options outstanding at the end of the year		1,844,871	9,345,331

In addition to the above options, parallel options over 2,195,124 ordinary shares at 152p per share were outstanding at 2nd January 1988.

20 Reserves

	Group	Company
	£m	£m
Share premium account		
At 3rd January 1987	121.1	121.1
On shares issued during the year	9.4	9.4
At 2nd January 1988	130.5	130.5
Revaluation and other reserves		
At 3rd January 1987	15.9	42.7
Guaranteed bond issue expenses	(0.2)	–
Release of revaluation surplus	(0.3)	–
At 2nd January 1988	15.4	42.7

Profit and loss account		
At 3rd January 1987	213.9	26.3
Exchange differences	(16.2)	–
Retained profit/(loss) for the year	44.3	(16.0)
Goodwill written off during the year	(2.7)	–
Release of revaluation surplus	0.3	–
	239.6	10.3

The amount of profit after extraordinary items but before dividends dealt with in the accounts of United Biscuits (Holdings) plc was £30.2m (1986 loss £12.2m).

21 Pay and benefits to employees

	1987	1986
	£m	£m
Gross wages and salaries, holiday and sick pay	**365.9**	369.0
Social security costs	**53.1**	50.2
Pension and other costs	**23.6**	24.5
	442.6	443.7

22 Disposal and acquisition of businesses

	Disposal		Acquisition	
	1987	1986	**1987**	1986
	£m	£m	**£m**	£m
Net assets disposed or acquired				
Tangible assets	**3.2**	–	–	0.4
Goodwill arising (charged to reserves)	**–**	–	–	1.0
Net current assets	**2.4**	–	–	0.3
	5.6	–	–	1.7
Interest received	**0.2**	–	–	–
Financed by issue of shares	**–**	–	–	(0.5)
Cash proceeds or payment	**5.8**	–	–	1.2

£1.1m of the cash proceeds were received in March 1988.

23 Change in working capital

	1987	1986
	£m	£m
Increase/(decrease):		
Stocks	**(7.1)**	9.0
Debtors	**2.9**	(18.2)
	(4.2)	(9.2)
Creditors	**10.0**	34.7
	5.8	(43.9)

24 Directors' interests in the share capital of the company

	Beneficial		As trustee		Options	
	1987	1986	**1987**	1986	**1987**	1986
Ordinary shares						
Executive						
Sir Hector Laing	**1,722,590**	1,752,590	**1,634,484**	1,734,484	**70,232**	297,472
R C Clarke	**12,000**	3,000	–	–	**236,557**	231,647
J Blyth	**20,704**	12,720	–	–	**152,861**	174,439
T M Garvin	**2,000**	2,000	–	–	**40,816**	40,816
F W Knight	**2,000**	–	–	–	**278,105**	261,955
D R J Stewart	**10,000**	8,927	–	–	**99,663**	100,636

Non-Executive						
E L Bondy Jnr	**3,273**	3,273	–	–	–	–
Sir James Cleminson	**2,200**	2,200	**413**	413	–	–
C A Fraser	**18,024**	18,024	**1,790,872**	1,910,872	–	–
W P Gunn	**103,994**	103,994	–	–	**68,270**	70,066
M A Heller	**1,106,392**	1,156,392	**1,024,254**	1,024,254	–	–
Rt Hon Sir Michael Palliser	**3,000**	3,000	–	–	–	–
Lord Plumb	**3,120**	3,120	–	–	–	–
Rt Hon Lord Prior	**31,243**	36,243	–	–	–	–

1,234,484 ordiniary shares are duplicated under trustee holdings (1986 1,364,484).

The options are exercisable at prices varying from $128\frac{1}{2}$p to 282p up to April 1997.

The directors have no interest in the loan capital of the company.

25 Emoluments of directors and senior employees

	1987 £000	1986 £000
Fees as directors	**87**	81
Emoluments as executives	**1,828**	1,137
Pensions in respect of former directors	**200**	227
Ex-gratia payment to former director	**–**	60
	2,115	1,505
Emoluments (excluding pension fund contributions) of the chairman	**162**	141
Emoluments (excluding pension fund contributions) of the highest paid director	**224**	154

Emoluments	**Directors**		**Employees**	
£	**1987**	1986	**1987**	1986
0 – 5,000	**–**	1		
5,001 – 10,000	**2**	4		
10,001 – 15,000	**3**	1		
15,001 – 20,000	**3**	2		
30,001 – 35,000	**–**	–	**55**	49
35,001 – 40,000	**–**	–	**34**	17

40,001 – 45,000	**–**	–	**16**	18
45,001 – 50,000	**–**	–	**8**	11
50,001 – 55,000	**–**	–	**9**	6
55,001 – 60,000	**–**	1	**7**	2
60,001 – 65,000	**–**	–	**4**	3
65,001 – 70,000	**–**	–	**4**	3
70,001 – 75,000	**–**	–	**4**	2
75,001 – 80,000	**1**	–	**1**	2
80,001 – 85,000	**–**	–	**2**	2
85,001 – 90,000	**–**	–	**1**	–
90,001 – 95,000	**–**	–	**2**	1
95,001 – 100,000	**–**	–	**2**	–
105,001 – 110,000	**–**	–	**1**	–
110,001 – 115,000	**–**	–	**1**	–
115,001 – 120,000	**–**	1	**–**	1
125,001 – 130,000	**–**	–	**1**	–
165,001 – 170,000	**1**	–	**–**	–
190,001 – 195,000	**1**	–	**–**	–
Directors, included above, for part of the year only	**2**	–		
Directors performing duties mainly outside the UK	**1**	1		

As at 2nd January 1988 R C Clarke had an interest free loan from the company amounting to £25,000 (1986 £25,000) repayable on his leaving the group.

26 Contingent liabilities

	Group		Company	
	1987	1986	**1987**	1986
	£m	£m	**£m**	£m
Guarantees given under the group's house purchase scheme (including £3,900 in respect of D R J Stewart, a director)	**0.2**	0.2	**0.2**	0.2
Guarantees by the company of subsidiaries' borrowings (mainly foreign currency)	–	–	**110.4**	198.5
Contingent liability under VAT group election	–	–	**7.0**	7.8
	0.2	0.2	**117.6**	206.5

27 Litigation

The Procter & Gamble Company ("P&G"), having obtained a patent in the USA in respect of a soft cookie product, has brought patent infringement and unfair competition claims in the US courts against Keebler Company ("Keebler"), a wholly owned subsidiary of the company, in respect of its "Soft Batch" cookie range. P&G is seeking an injunction against the manufacture and sale by Keebler of products allegedly violating its patent, although for more than a year Keebler's production of this range of products is conceded by P&G not to violate its patent. P&G in addition seeks monetary damages which have not been quantified. While the allegations are being refuted and the action is being strongly defended, at the instigation of the Court preliminary settlement discussions have been held, thus far unsuccessfully. In the opinion of the directors the results of this litigation will not have a significant effect on the group's financial position. Similar claims have been brought by P&G against two other companies which manufactured soft cookies, Nabisco Brands Inc. and Frito-Lay, Inc.

23 Financial commitments

The group's financial commitments at the year-end in respect of finance lease and hire purchase obligations and in respect of its pension commitments are set out in notes 17 and 18 respectively. The group's financial commitments in respect of capital expenditure and rentals are summarised below:

	1987	1986
	£m	£m
Capital expenditure – contracted for	**23.0**	22.1
– authorised but not contracted for	**15.7**	20.8

Rental commitments

As at 2nd January 1988 the group had annual rental commitments in respect of operating leases as follows:

	1987		1986	
	Land & buildings	**Other**	Land & buildings	Other
	£m	**£m**	£m	£m
Expiring – within one year	**0.9**	**0.8**	0.6	0.5
– over one year and under five years	**3.1**	**4.8**	3.4	5.3
– after five years	**20.6**	**0.3**	19.9	0.7
	24.6	**5.9**	23.9	6.5

In addition to the rental commitments set out above, the group held the head-lease to 290 properties (1986 236) which were sub-let to third parties. The group had no net rental commitments in respect of such properties, on which gross head-lease rents of £7.4m arose during the year (1986 £5.8m).

Report of the Auditors

to the members of United Biscuits (Holdings) plc

We have audited the accounts on pages 32 to 49 in accordance with approved auditing standards.

In our opinion the accounts, which have been prepared on the basis of the accounting policies on page 36, give a true and fair view of the state of affairs of the company and the group at 2nd January 1988 and of the profit and source and application of funds of the group for the fifty-two weeks then ended, and comply with the Companies Act 1985.

Deloitte Haskins & Sells	Arthur Young
Chartered Accountants	*Chartered Accountants*
London	London

30th March 1988

Group statistics

	1987 £m	1986 £m	1985 £m	1984 £m	1983 £m
Summarised results					
Turnover	**1,954.6**	1,932.5	1,907.2	1,743.1	1,424.7
Trading profit (1)	**157.6**	138.0	122.7	110.6	99.4
Trading profit as a percentage of turnover	**8.1%**	7.1%	6.4%	6.3%	7.0%
Profit before taxation (1)	**147.0**	125.2	102.2	87.2	83.3
Profit before taxation as a percentage of turnover	**7.5%**	6.5%	5.4%	5.0%	5.8%
Profit attributable to shareholders	**98.4**	82.6	71.0	62.4	57.7
Earnings per share (2)	**23.9p**	20.3p	19.1p	19.1p	17.9p
Dividends per share (2)	**11.0p**	9.5p	8.0p	7.3p	6.8p
Net assets					
Fixed assets	**564.4**	538.6	483.7	497.8	398.1
Net current assets	**111.4**	170.0	147.8	51.6	70.0
	675.8	708.6	631.5	549.4	468.1
Loans and finance leases	**154.7**	231.2	201.2	222.2	170.8
Other non-current creditors	**30.6**	23.8	15.8	25.5	38.6
	490.5	453.6	414.5	301.7	258.7

Financed by					
Share capital	**104.0**	102.0	101.6	79.9	78.8
Reserves (including minorities)	**386.5**	351.6	312.9	221.8	179.9
	490.5	453.6	414.5	301.7	258.7
Net assets per share	**118p**	111p	102p	92p	80p

(1) The results for 1983 have been restated to reflect the changed accounting policy in respect of foreign currency translations.

(2) Earnings per share and dividends per share for 1984 and 1983 have been adjusted for the bonus element of the rights issue in March 1985.

Financial calendar

Results

Half year results	Announced 16th September 1987
Full year results	Announced 16th March 1988
Report and accounts	Posted 12th April 1988
Annual general meeting	Edinburgh 5th May 1988

Dividend payments

– Interim	Announced 16th September 1987 Paid 6th January 1988

– Final	Proposed 16th March 1988 Payable 1st July 1988

Analysis of shareholders

At 2nd January 1988

	No. of holders	No. of shares 000's	% of share capital
Individuals	21,262	56,820	13.7
Trustee and joint holders	516	7,991	1.9
Banks and nominee companies	2,648	228,187	54.9
Insurance companies	245	57,074	13.7
Investment companies	86	4,676	1.1
Pension funds	80	15,352	3.7
Other companies	651	23,064	5.5
Others	276	22,782	5.5
	25,764	415,946	100.0

Analysis of individual shareholders

Shares held	No. of holders	% of all holders	No. of shares 000's	% of share capital
1 – 1,000	9,581	37.2	5,576	1.4
1,001 – 5,000	10,307	40.0	22,233	5.4
5,001 – 20,000	1,204	4.6	10,455	2.5
20,001 – 50,000	101	0.4	3,003	0.7
Over 50,000	69	0.3	15,553	3.7
	21,262	82.5	56,820	13.7

Taxation

The sale of shares or stock by a shareholder or stockholder may give rise to a tax liability in respect of capital gains. For sales occurring on or after 6th April 1985 (1st April 1985 for companies) the market value of the shares or stock at 31st March 1982 may be relevant.

The respective market values were as follows:

Ordinary shares	122.20p†
8% debenture stock 1993/98	£62.25
$5\frac{1}{4}$% unsecured loan stock 2003/08	£38.25

† Adjusted for the rights issue in March 1985.

12 Accounts in Other Countries

We are now going to take a look at the accounting statements common in the USA and list some of the common accounting terms used in French and German accounts.

12.1 **American Balance Sheets**

As with the British balance sheet, there are a variety of ways in which the American one can be presented. We noted the way the balance sheet is set out in the USA on p. 40. Check back to remind yourself of the two ways in which it differs from the British methods.

The other main difference is in the terms that are actually used. You will find an American balance sheet set out below with the British 'translation' in brackets after the American words:

Assets

	$ million
Current assets	
Cash	105
Marketable securities at cost (investments)	70
Accounts receivable, or receivables (debtors)	295
Inventories (stocks)	400
Total current assets	870
Fixed assets	
Land and buildings	4 600
Machinery and equipment	1 400
	6 000
Less accumulated depreciation	3 800
Net fixed assets	2 200
Prepayments	100
Intangibles (goodwill, patents, trademarks)	30
Total assets	$3 200

Liabilities and net worth	
	$ million
Current liabilities	
Notes payable (overdrafts, etc.)	50
Accounts payable (creditors)	250
Income taxes payable	200
Dividends payable	50
Total current liabilities	550
Long-term liabilities	300
Total liabilities (or debt)	850
Stockholders equity	
Preferred stock (preference shares)	650
Common stock (ordinary shares)	1 000
Capital surplus (share premium)	200
Acumulated retained earnings (retained profits)	500
Total net worth (equity capital)	2 350
Total liabilities and stockholders equity (total capital)	$3 200

12.2 **Profit and Loss Account USA Style**

The US system for determining profit is much the same as in Britain. However, there are some differences – mainly in the words used. Indeed, the statement is usually called 'the income statement' and its layout follows the lines of Format 1:

	$ millions	
Net sales	100	
Cost of sales and operating expenses	80	
Operating income	20	
Other income	2	
Total income	22	(or earnings before interest and tax (EBIT))
Less interest on bonds	6	
Income before tax	16	
Income tax provision	7	
Net income or earnings for year	9	
Less dividends on preferred stock and common stock	4	
Retained earnings for year	$ 5	

12.3 Summary of French and German Accounting Terms

English	*French*	*German*
Sales	Ventes	Verkäufe
Profit before tax	Bénéfice avant Impôts	Gewinn vor Steuern
Tax	Impôts	Steuern
Depreciation	Amortissement	Abschreibungen
Dividends	Dividendes	Dividenden
Retained profit	Bénéfice non distribué	Nicht ausgeschütteter Gewinn
Balance sheet	Bilan	Bilanz
Assets	Actifs	Aktiva
Stocks	Stocks	Warenbestände
Debtors	Débiteurs	Schuldner, Debitor
Current assets	Actif circulant	Umlaufvermögen
Investments	Participations	Beteiligungen
Fixed assets	Immobilisa-tions	Anlagevermögen
		Geschäftswerk
Goodwill	Fonds de commerce	

Shareholders' funds	Capital propre réserves et bénéfices non distribués	Eigencapital
Loan capital	Capitaux empruntés	Darlehen
Capital employed	Fonds utilisés	Kapitalherkunft

Glossary of Accounting Terms

asset An item of value.

audit Examination of an organisation's affairs, mainly through its accounting records.

authorised share capital The total number and value of shares that a company can issue, as set out in its **memorandum of association**.

balance sheet A statement showing the assets held by a company, their value and the sources of its finances at a point in time.

book value The accounting value of an asset.

book-keeping The techniques of recording financial transactions.

borrowed capital The finance of a company that has to be paid back to the lender.

capital employed The funds used by a company to acquire assets.

capital structure The way a company has raised its long-term finance, through borrowing or **equity capital**.

company A legal organisation set up by registration under the Companies Acts, or by Act of Parliament or by charter, and having a life independent of its members.

company limited by shares A company where the members are liable for the company's debts only to the amount they owe on their shares.

consolidated accounts Accounting statements where the accounts of a holding company and all its subsidiaries are amalgamated into one, as though it were a single entity.

convertible loan stock A loan which entitles the holder to change to ordinary shares, usually at a set time.

cost of sales The expenses associated with sales turnover, including **overheads** and the **direct costs**.

creditor A person or organisation to whom money is owed and (in the balance sheet) the total of such sums.

cumulative preference shares Shares entitling the holder to a fixed rate of dividend, before the ordinary shareholders and any arrears are made up in future years.

current asset The assets used in a company's day-to-day trading activities; includes cash, debtors and stocks.

current cost accounting (CCA) A system of accounting where assets are included at their present-day values rather than the cost at which they were obtained. Profits are adjusted to reflect these higher values.

current liabilities Amounts of money owed by a company which have to be paid in the near future, normally within a year; includes creditors, bank overdrafts, current tax due and dividends due.

debentures A source of borrowing for a company, of a long-term nature and usually stating the rate of interest and when repayment is to occur.

debt The total amount owed by a company.

debt capacity The total amount of finance a company could in theory borrow.

debtor An individual or organisation who owed money to a company and (in the balance sheet) the sum of money owed in this way.

depreciation The permanent loss of value of an asset from whatever cause.

direct cost of sales The sum of materials used, direct wages, and direct expenses associated with the item sold.

dividend cover Earnings per share *divided by* dividends per share.

dividend yield Dividend per share *divided by* current share price.

dividends The money paid out of profits to shareholders.

EBIT Earnings before interest and tax.

earnings Profit after deducting interest charges, tax, minority interests, and preference dividends, but before deducting extraordinary items.

earnings per share (EPS) Earnings *divided by* the number of issued ordinary shares.

equity capital The net worth of a business, or the capital belonging to the ordinary shareholders; includes issued share capital, reserves and profits retained in the company.

financial structure The way a company's total finances have been arranged.

fixed assets A valuable item in an organisation of a lasting nature and not used up in the trading process; includes land, buildings, machinery and vehicles.

gearing The proportion of a company's capital that has been borrowed or is **equity**.

goodwill The excess price paid for a business over its **book value**.

gross profit Turnover less cost of sales (q.v.).

historical cost The actual cost of obtaining an asset, or goods or services.

insolvency The inability to meet debts that are due.

intangible asset An asset that does not have a physical appearance.

interest The sum of money paid by a borrower to a lender for the use of money.

interest cover Profit before interest and tax *divided by* all interest paid out.

issued share capital The number and amount of shares issued to ordinary shareholders.

lease An asset hired rather than bought, on which rent is paid.
liabilities The financial obligations of a company.
liquid assets Assets that can be turned quickly into money.
loan capital Finance that has been borrowed and not obtained from the shareholders.
memorandum of association The document that contains the basis of the legal constitution of a company.
net worth The sum of a company's paid-up share capital and reserves (including retained profits).
overheads Costs incurred other than direct costs, i.e. not charged directly to the product sold.
participating preference shares Shares with a fixed dividend and the possibility of a share of remaining profits if adequate.
payments in advance Sums paid out in one year for the benefit of a future period. A current asset.
preference shares Shares that have a fixed rate of dividend and which are paid before ordinary shareholders' entitlement.
price/earnings ratio (P/E) The current market price of a share *divided by* **earnings per share**.
private company A company with at least two members, has the word 'Limited' or 'Ltd' after its name and is not a **public company**.
productivity Quantity of output in relation to input; often output per employee.
profit See **trading profit** and **earnings**.
profit and loss account A statement showing what profit has been made over a period and the uses to which the profit has been put.
profitability The measure of how effectively a company has been operating. Obtained by: profits *divided by* assets or capital employed.
public limited company (plc) A company limited by shares, has a share capital, has at least two members, is registered under the Companies Acts and has the letters 'plc' after its name (in Wales the letters 'ccc' will be found).
reserves Part of equity capital and consisting of **retained profits**, surplus values created by the revaluation of assets, and other surplus sums arising from the sale of shares.
retained profit Profits kept in the company after all commitments have been met and shareholders paid a dividend.
rights issue An issue of extra shares to existing shareholders in proportion to their existing holding, often at a favourable price.
risk The probability that the return on an investment will not be as expected. Refers also to the probability of any future event turning out worse than anticipated.

sales The total value of goods and services sold outside during a period.

scrip issue (or bonus issue) An issue of extra shares to existing shareholders at no cost in proportion to their existing holding. The total amount involved is transferred from reserves to issued share capital and is known as the 'capitalization' of reserves'.

share capital The shareholders' investment in a company (see also **issued share capital**).

share premium The excess paid for a share, to the company, over its nominal value.

source and application of funds A statement showing the sources of money in a company during a period and the uses to which that money has been put.

Statement of Standard Accounting Practice (SSAP) The accountancy bodies' recommendations for good practice in accounting matters in the United Kingdom.

stock (1) Items held for conversion at a later date into sales, including materials, finished goods, components, bought-out parts and **work in progress**. Included in current assets.

stock (2) A fixed amount of paid-up capital held by a stockholder. Also, in USA, the equivalent of shares.

tangible assets Assets that have a physical identity.

trading profit Profit from the operations of the business: gross profit *less* **overhead costs**.

turnover Revenues from the sale of goods or services, usually after deducting any sales or value added taxes and duties, trade discounts, and goods returned.

value added The sum of wages costs, depreciation and profit *equals* sales *less* cost of materials and other bought-out goods and services.

work in progress Items held that are not in their original state, but which have been partly made ready for sale.

working capital The capital available on a day-to-day basis for the operations of the business, which consists of current assets *less* current liabilities.

Further Reading

A Guide to Financial Times Statistics. Financial Times Business Information, 1987.

Ingham, H. and Taylor Harrington, L. *Interfirm Comparison*. Heinemann, 1980.

Lewis, Pendrill *et al. Advanced Financial Accounting*. Pitman, 1981.

Management Accounting Official Terminology. Institute of Cost and Management Accountants, 1982.

Sizer, J. *An Insight into Management Accounting*. Penguin, 1982.

Weston and Brigham, *Managerial Finance*. Holt, Rinehart & Winston, 1979.

Westwick, C. A. *How to Use Management Ratios*. Gower, 1987.

Harraps French and English Business Dictionary.

Freidrich K. Feldbausch, *Financial Dictionary* (English/German). Leviathan House, 1972.

If you want to see a company's accounts, write to the company secretary at their head office, or reply to the advertisement which the company will have placed in the financial pages of the press when its results were announced.

Specific statistics on company performance will be found in various issues of *Management Today* and the *Financial Times*. The American magazine *Fortune* publishes a very detailed set of profitability league tables called the *Fortune 500* each May, and also a world league table later in the year.

APPENDIX

Schedule 4 to the Companies Act 1985

Section 1

SCHEDULE 4

ACCOUNTS

PART 1

Basic Requirements with Respect to the Form and Content of a Company's Accounts

SECTION A

General Rules with Respect to the Form and Content of Accounts

1.—(1) Subject to the following provisions of this Schedule—
(*a*) every balance sheet of a company shall show the items listed in either of the balance sheet formats set out below in section B of this Part; and
(*b*) every profit and loss account of a company shall show the items listed in any one of the profit and loss account formats so set out;

in either case in the order and under the headings and sub-headings given in the format adopted.

(2) Sub-paragraph (1) above shall not be read as requiring the heading or sub-heading for any item to be distinguished by any letter or number assigned to that item in the format adopted.

2(1) Where in accordance with paragraph 1 above a company's balance sheet or profit and loss account for any financial year has been prepared by reference to one of the formats set out in section B below, the directors of the company shall adopt the same format in preparing the accounts for subsequent financial years of the company unless in their opinion there are special reasons for a change.

(2) Particulars of any change in the format adopted in preparing a company's balance sheet or profit and loss account in accordance with paragraph 1 above shall be disclosed, and the reasons for the change shall be explained, in a note to the accounts in which the new format is first adopted.

3(1) Any item required in accordance with paragraph 1 above to be shown in a company's balance sheet or profit and loss account may be shown in greater detail than required by the format adopted.

(2) A company's balance sheet or profit and loss account may include an item representing or covering the amount of any asset or liability, income or expenditure not otherwise covered by any of the items listed in the format adopted, but the following shall not be treated as assets in any company's balance sheet—

(*a*) preliminary expenses;

(*b*) expenses of and commission on any issue of shares or debentures; and

(*c*) costs of research

(3) In preparing a company's balance sheet or profit and loss account the directors of the company shall adapt the arrangement and headings and sub-headings otherwise required by paragraph 1 above in respect of items to which an Arabic number is assigned in the format adopted, in any case where the special nature of the company's business requires such adaptation.

(4) Items to which Arabic numbers are assigned in any of the formats set out in section B below may be combined in a company's accounts for any financial year if either—

(*a*) their individual amounts are not material to assessing the state of affairs or profit or loss of the company for that year; or

(*b*) the combination facilitates that assessment;

but in a case within paragraph (*b*) above the individual amounts of any items so combined shall be disclosed in a note to the accounts.

(5) Subject to paragraph 4 (3) below, a heading or sub-heading corresponding to an item listed in the format adopted in preparing a company's balance sheet or profit and loss account shall not be included if there is no amount to be shown for that item in respect of the financial year to which the balance sheet or profit and loss account relates.

(6) Every profit and loss account of a company shall show the amount of the company's profit or loss on ordinary activities before taxation.

(7) Every profit and loss account of a company shall show separately as additional items—

(*a*) any amount set aside or proposed to be set aside to, or withdrawn or proposed to be withdrawn from, reserves; and

(*b*) the aggregate amount of any dividends paid and proposed.

4(1) In respect of every item shown in a company's balance sheet or profit and loss account the corresponding amount for the financial year immediately preceding that to which the balance sheet or profit and loss account relates shall also be shown.

(2) Where that corresponding amount is not comparable with the amount to be shown for the item in question in respect of the financial year to which the balance sheet or profit and loss account relates, the former amount shall be adjusted and particulars of the adjustment and the reasons for it shall be disclosed in a note to the accounts.

(3) Paragraph 3 (5) above shall not apply in any case where an amount can be shown for the item in question in respect of the financial year immediately preceding that to which the balance sheet or profit and loss account relates, and that amount shall be shown under the heading or sub-heading required by paragraph 1 above for that item.

5. Amounts in respect of items representing assets or income may not be set off against amounts in respect of items representing liabilities or expenditure (as the case may be), or vice versa.

SECTION B

The Required Formats for Accounts

Preliminary

6. References in this Part of this Schedule to the items listed in any of the formats set out below are references to those items read together with any of the notes following the formats which apply to any of those items, and the requirement imposed by paragraph 1 above to show the items listed in any such format in the order adopted in the format is subject to any provision in those notes for alternative positions for any particular items.

7. A number in brackets following any item in any of the formats set out below is a reference to the note of that number in the notes following the formats.

8. In the notes following the formats—

(*a*) the heading of each note gives the required heading or sub-heading for the item to which it applies and a reference to any letters and numbers assigned to that item in the formats set out below (taking a reference in the case of Format 2 of the balance sheet formats to the item listed under "Assets" or under "Liabilities" as the case may require); and (*b*) references to a numbered format are references to the balance sheet format or (as the case may require) to the profit and loss account format of that number set out below.

Balance Sheet Formats

Format 1

A. Called up share capital not paid (*1*)
B. Fixed assets
  I Intangible assets
    1. Development costs
    2. Concessions, patents, licences, trade marks and similar rights and assets (*2*)
    3. Goodwill (*3*)
    4. Payments on account
  II Tangible assets
    1. Land and buildings
    2. Plant and machinery
    3. Fixtures, fittings, tools and equipment
    4. Payments on account and assets in course of construction
  III Investments
    1. Shares in group companies
    2. Loans to group companies
    3. Shares in related companies
    4. Loans to related companies
    5. Other investments other than loans
    6. Other loans
    7. Own shares (*4*)
C. Current assets
  I Stocks
    1. Raw materials and consumables
    2. Work in progress
    3. Finished goods and goods for resale
    4. Payments on account
  II Debtors (*5*)
    1. Trade debtors
    2. Amounts owed by group companies
    3. Amounts owed by related companies
    4. Other debtors
    5. Called up share capital not paid (*1*)
    6. Prepayments and accrued income (*6*)

III Investments
   1. Shares in group companies
   2. Own shares (*4*)
   3. Other investments

IV Cash at bank and in hand

D. Prepayment and accrued income (*6*)

E. Creditors; amounts falling due within one year
   1. Debenture loans (*7*)
   2. Bank loans and overdrafts
   3. Payments received on account (*8*)
   4. Trade creditors
   5. Bills of exchange payable
   6. Amounts owed to group companies
   7. Amounts owed to related companies
   8. Other creditors including taxation and social security (*9*)
   9. Accruals and deferred income (*10*)

F. Net current assets (liabilities) (*11*)

G. Total assets less current liabilities

H. Creditors; amounts falling due after more than one year
   1. Debenuture loans (*7*)
   2. Bank loans and overdrafts
   3. Payments received on account (*8*)
   4. Trade creditors
   5. Bills of exchange payable
   6. Amounts owed to group companies
   7. Amounts owed to related companies
   8. Other creditors including taxation and social security (*9*)
   9. Accruals and deferred income (*10*)

I. Provisions for liabilities and charges
   1. Pensions and similar obligations
   2. Taxation, including deferred taxation
   3. Other provisions

J. Accruals and deferred income (*10*)

K. Capital and reserves

I Called up share capital (*12*)

II Share premium account

III Revaluation reserve

IV Other reserves
   1. Capital redemption reserve
   2. Reserve for own shares
   3. Reserves provided for by the articles of association
   4. Other reserves

V profit and loss account

Balance Sheet Formats

Format 2

ASSETS

A. Called up share capital not paid (*1*)

B. Fixed assets

I Intangible assets

1. Development costs
2. Concessions, patents, licences, trade marks and similar rights and assets (*2*)
3. Goodwill (*3*)
4. Payments on account

II Tangible asssets

1. Land and buildings
2. Plant and machinery
3. Fixtures, fittings, tools and equipment
4. Payments on account and assets in course of construction

III Investments

1. Shares in group companies
2. Loans to group companies
3. Shares in related companies
4. Loans to related companies
5. Other investments other than loans
6. Other loans
7. Own shares (*4*)

C. Current assets

I Stocks

1. Raw materials and consumables
2. Work in progress
3. Finished goods and goods for resale
4. Payments on account

II Debtors (*5*)

1. Trade debtors
2. Amounts owed by group companies
3. Amounts owed by related companies
4. Other debtors
5. Called up share capital not paid (*1*)
6. Prepayments and accrued income (*6*)

III Investments

1. Shares in group companies
2. Own shares (*4*)
3. Other investments

IV Cash at bank and in hand

D. Prepayments and accrued income (*6*)

LIABILITIES

A. Capital and reserves
  - I Called up share capital (*12*)
  - II Share premium account
  - III Revaluation reserve
  - IV Other reserves
    1. Capital redemption reserve
    2. Reserve for own shares
    3. Reserves provided for by the articles of association
    4. Other reserves
  - V Profit and loss account

B. Provisions for liabilities and charges
  1. Pensions and similar obligations
  2. Taxation, including deferred taxation
  3. Other provisions

C. Creditors (*13*)
  1. Debenture loans (*7*)
  2. Bank loans and overdrafts
  3. Payments received on account (*8*)
  4. Trade creditors
  5. Bills of exchange payable
  6. Amounts owed to group companies
  7. Amounts owed to related companies
  8. Other creditors including taxation and social security (*9*)
  9. Accruals and deferred income (*10*)

D. Accruals and deferred income (*10*)

Notes on the balance sheet formats

(*1*) *Called up share capital not paid*

(Formats 1 and 2, items A and C.II.5.)

This item may be shown in either of the two positions given in Formats 1 and 2.

(*2*) Concessions, patents, licences, trade marks and similar rights and assets

(Formats 1 and 2, item B.I.2.)

Amounts in respect of assets shall only be included in a company's balance sheet under this item if either—

(*a*) the assets were acquired for valuable consideration and are not required to be shown under goodwill; or

(*b*) the assets in question were created by the company itself.

(3) *Goodwill*

(Formats 1 and 2, item B.I.3.)

Amounts representing goodwill shall only be included to the extent that the goodwill was acquired for valuable consideration.

(4) *Own shares*

(Formats 1 and 2, items B.III.7 and C.III.2.)

The nominal value of the shares held shall be shown separately.

(5) *Debtors*

(Formats 1 and 2, items C.II.1 to 6.)

The amount falling due after more than one year shall be shown separately for each item included under debtors.

(6) *Prepayments and accrued income*

(Formats 1 and 2, items C.II.6 and D.)

This item may be shown in either of the two positions given in Formats 1 and 2.

(7) *Debenture loans*

(Formats 1, items E.1 and H.1 and Formats 2, item C.1.)

The amount of any convertible loans shall be shown separately.

(8) *Payments received on account*

(Formats 1, items E.3 and H.3 and Formats 2, items C.3.)

Payments received on account of orders shall be shown for each or these items in so far as they are not shown as deductions from stocks.

(9) *Other creditors including taxation and social security.*

(Formats 1, items E.8 and H.8 and Format 2, item C.8.)

The amount for creditors in respect of taxation and social security shall be shown separately from the amount for other creditors.

(10) *Accruals and deferred income*

(Formats 1, items E.9, H.9 and J and Format 2, items C.9 and D.)

The two positions given for this item in Format 1 at E.9 and H.9 are an alternative to the position at J but if the item is not shown in a position corresponding to that at J it may be shown in either or both of the other two positions (as the case may require).

The two positions given for this item in Format 2 are alternatives.

(11) *Net current assets (liabilities)*

(Format 1, item F.)

In determining the amount to be shown for this item any amount shown under "prepayments and accrued income" shall be taken into account wherever shown.

(12) *Called up share capital*

(Format 1, item K.1 and Format 2, item A.I.)

The amount of allotted share capital and the amount of called up share capital which has been paid up shall be shown separately.

(*13*) *Creditors*

(Formats 2, items C.1 to 9.)

Amounts falling due within one year and after one year shall be shown separately for each of these items and their aggregate shall be shown separately for all of these items.

Profit and loss account formats

Format 1

(see note (17) below

1. Turnover
2. Cost of sales (*14*)
3. Gross profit or loss
4. Distribution costs (*14*)
5. Administrative expenses (*14*)
6. Other operating income
7. Income from shares in group companies
8. Income from shares in related companies
9. Income from other fixed asset investments (*15*)
10. Other interest receivable and similar income (*15*)
11. Amounts written off investments
12. Interest payable and similar charges (*16*)
13. Tax on profit or loss on ordinary activities
14. Profit or loss on ordinary activities after taxation
15. Extraordinary income
16. Extraordinary charges
17. Extraordinary profit or loss
18. Tax on extraordinary profit or loss
19. Other taxes not shown under the above items
20. Profit or loss for the financial year

Profit and loss account formats

Format 2

1. Turnover
2. Change in stocks of finished goods and in work progress
3. Own work capitalised
4. Other operating income
5. (*a*) Raw materials and consumables
   (*b*) Other external charges

6. Staff costs:
   (*a*) wages and salaries
   (*b*) social security costs
   (*c*) other pension costs
7. (*a*) Depreciation and other amounts written off tangible and intangible fixed assets
   (*b*) Exceptional amounts written off current assets
8. Other operating charges
9. Income from shares in group companies
10. Income from shares in related companies
11. Income from other fixed asset investments (*15*)
12. Other interest receivable and similar income (*15*)
13. Amounts written off investments
14. Interest payable and similar charges (*16*)
15. Tax on profit or loss on ordinary activities
16. Profit or loss on ordinary activities after taxation
17. Extraordinary income
18. Extraordinary charges
19. Extraordinary profit or loss
20. Tax on extraordinary profit or loss
21. Other taxes not shown under the above items
22. Profit or loss for the financial year

Profit and loss acount formats

Format 3

(see note (*17*) below)

A. Charges
   1. Cost of sales (*14*)
   2. Distribution costs (*14*)
   3. Administrative expenses (*14*)
   4. Amounts written off investments
   5. Interest payable and similar charges (*16*)
   6. Tax on profit or loss on ordinary activities
   7. Profit or loss on ordinary activities after taxation
   8. Extraordinary charges
   9. Tax on extraordinary profit or loss
   10. Other taxes not shown under the above items
   11. Profit or loss for the financial year

B. Income
   1. Turnover
   2. Other operating income

3. Income from shares in group companies
4. Income from shares in related companies
5. Income from other fixed asset investments (*15*)
6. Other interest receivable and similar income (*15*)
7. Profit or loss on ordinary activities after taxation
8. Extraordinary income
9. Profit or loss for the financial year

Profit and loss account formats

Format 4

A. Charges
   1. Reduction in stocks of finished goods and in work in progress
   2. (*a*) Raw materials and consumables
      (*b*) Other external charges
   3. Staff costs:
      (*a*) wages and salaries
      (*b*) social security costs
      (*c*) other pension costs
   4. (*a*) Depreciation and other amounts written off tangible and intangible fixed assets.
      (*b*) Exceptional amounts written off current assets
   5. Other operating charges
   6. Amounts written off investments
   7. Interest payable and similar charges (*16*)
   8. Tax on profit or loss on ordinary activities
   9. Profit or loss on ordinary activities after taxation
   10. Extraordinary charges
   11. Tax on extraordinary profit or loss
   12. Other taxes not shown under the above items
   13. Profit or loss for the financial year

B. Income
   1. Turnover
   2. Increase in stocks of finished goods and in work in progress
   3. Own work capitalised
   4. Other operating income
   5. Income from shares in group companies
   6. Income from shares in related companies
   7. Income from other fixed asset investments (*15*)
   8. Other interest receivable and similar income (*15*)
   9. Profit or loss on ordinary activities after taxation
   10. Extraordinary income
   11. Profit or loss for the financial year

Notes on the profit and loss account formats

(*14*) *Cost of sales: distribution costs: administrative expenses*
(Format 1, items 2, 4 and 5 and Format 3, items A.2, 2 and 3.)
These items shall be stated after taking into account any necessary provisions for depreciation or diminution in value of assets.

(*15*) *Income from other fixed asset investments: other interest receivable and similar income*
(Format 1, items 9 and 10; Format 2, items 11 and 12: Format 3, items B.5 and 6: Format 4, items B.7 and 8.)
Income and interest derived from group companies shall be shown separately from income and interest derived from other sources.

(*16*) *Interest payable and similar charges*
(Format 1, item 12: Format 2, item 14: Format 3, item A.5: Format 4, item A.7.)
The amount payable to group companies shall be shown separately.

(*17*) *Formats 1 and 3*
The amount of any provisions for depreciation and diminution in value of tangible and intangible fixed assets failing to be shown under items 7(*a*) and A.4(*a*) respectively in Formats 2 and 4 shall be disclosed in a note to the accounts in any case where the profit and loss account is prepared by reference to Format 1 or Format 3.

Index

Also available in the Macmillan Professional Masters series

MARGARET ATTWOOD
Personnel Management is the ideal book for those studying for professional and business exams, especially the Institute of Personnel Management and BTEC National level courses. It will also be useful for the personnel management elements of other management, business and psychology courses and a handy reference for practising managers.

JOHN BINGHAM
Data Processing is self-contained and up to date, and is ideal for relevant business and accounting courses or anyone who wishes to improve their existing knowledge and skills.

CHRIS BREWSTER
Employee Relations is a comprehensive and readable explanation of the parties, institutions and systems which are involved in the relationships between managers and employees. It is ideal for use on Institute of Industrial Management, Institute of Personnel Management and NEBBS courses and for all practising managers who carry employee-relations responsibilities.

E.C. EYRE
Office Administration is suitable for all syllabuses in office administration and relevant parts of business administration and management courses. It is an invaluable text for students studying for the examinations of the Institute of Administrative Management, the Institute of Chartered Secretaries and Administrators, the Society of Company and Commercial Accountants, BTEC and NEBBS.

ROGER HUSSEY
Cost and Management Accounting is a clear explanatory text covering the principles and techniques of the subject. It will prove invaluable for students in further and higher education, particularly those studying on accounting foundation, A-level and BTEC courses. It will also suit practising managers who wish to improve their existing skills.

ROBERT G.I. MAXWELL
Marketing is an invaluable introductory text for students of marketing, particularly those on BTEC, SCOTVEC, DMS and Certificate in Marketing courses. It will also prove a useful text for those studying A-Level Business Studies and for interested managers and those in the field of marketing and publicity.

ROGER OLDCORN
Management is a clear, accessible text which will appeal as a self-contained text to students on BTEC, SCOTVEC, Diploma in Management Studies and Institute of Personnel Management courses and as introductory reading for higher-level courses. It will also prove invaluable reading for practising or aspiring managers.

KATE WILLIAMS
Study Skills offers students practical, step-by-step suggestions and strategies to use in their studies, whether these are academic, professional or vocational in nature.